"A groundbreaking book on the lives of immigrant sex workers in Europe. Focused on West African women who work in window-prostitution rooms in Brussels and based on carefully conducted field observations and interviews, the book offers unique findings, insights, and policy recommendations regarding the women's lives, work, and struggles in a disadvantaged, crime-ridden part of the city that does not receive the police protection it deserves. A major contribution to our understanding of the lives of marginalized sex workers in Europe."

– Ronald Weitzer, Professor of Sociology,
George Washington University, USA

"A significant and important contribution to literature on trafficking of West African women to Europe. It provides a unique and insightful angle to the hidden perspective of trafficked women in prostitution, with narratives from the key informants, as these Nigerian and Ghanaian women share their experiences and challenges in red-light districts in Brussels."

– Kokunre Agbontaen-Eghafona, Professor of Anthropology,
University of Benin, Benin City, Nigeria

Nigerian and Ghanaian Women Working in the Brussels Red-Light District

This book unravels the lives, needs and experiences of Nigerian and Ghanaian women working in prostitution in Brussels.

This volume casts a light on the working conditions and the experiences of 38 women of Nigerian and Ghanaian origin, whose daily struggles and challenges are recalled from interviews in the field. Working within the red-light district of Brussels, an area with high crime rates and lacking in basic healthcare provision, the women are faced with a number of issues on a daily basis, ranging from security and health-related concerns, to work-related stress, discrimination and perceived stigma. Full voice is given to their stories, as well as contributions from state actors and local inhabitants, with the chief aim of building safe and healthy places for both residents and workers alike. The authors conclude in presenting clear recommendations and tools for practitioners and policy makers, designed to improve the outcomes of migrant women working not just within the red-light district of Brussels, but also within wider European and global contexts.

This book will be of particular interest for researchers and students of Migration Politics, Development Studies, Social Work and Sociology, as well as a useful guide for policy makers and practitioners in the field.

Sarah Adeyinka* is an Educational Sciences PhD candidate at Ghent University, Belgium. She has worked in the field of humanitarian aid for over a decade with a focus on vulnerable members of society such as refugees and survivors of human trafficking.

Sophie Samyn* is a PhD candidate in Social Work at Ghent University, Belgium. She worked for several years in migration centres in Italy and Belgium with migrants and unaccompanied minors who arrived (in Europe) through Libya and Greece.

Sami Zemni is a professor in political and social sciences at the Centre for Conflict and Development Studies, Ghent University, Belgium, where he coordinates and leads the Middle East and North Africa Research Group (MENARG).

Ilse Derluyn is a professor in the Department of Social Work and Social Pedagogy, Ghent University, Belgium where she coordinates the Centre for the Social Study of Migration and Refguees (CESSMIR).

* These authors contributed equally to the work.

Routledge Studies in Development, Mobilities and Migration

This series is dedicated to the growing and important area of mobilities and migration, particularly through the lens of international development. It promotes innovative and interdisciplinary research targeted at a global readership. The series welcomes submissions from established and junior authors on cutting-edge and high-level research on key topics that feature in global news and public debate.

These include the so called European migration crisis; famine in the Horn of Africa; riots; environmental migration; development-induced displacement and resettlement; livelihood transformations; people-trafficking; health and infectious diseases; employment; South-South migration; population growth; children's wellbeing; marriage and family; food security; the global financial crisis; drugs wars; and other contemporary crisis.

For more information about this series, please visit: https://www.routledge.com/Routledge-Studies-in-Development-Mobilities-and-Migration/book-series/RSDM.

Nigerian and Ghanaian Women Working in the Brussels Red-Light District

Sarah Adeyinka, Sophie Samyn,
Sami Zemni and Ilse Derluyn

Routledge
Taylor & Francis Group

LONDON AND NEW YORK

First published 2021
by Routledge
2 Park Square, Milton Park, Abingdon, Oxon OX14 4RN

and by Routledge
52 Vanderbilt Avenue, New York, NY 10017

Routledge is an imprint of the Taylor & Francis Group, an informa business

British Library Cataloguing in Publication Data
A catalogue record for this book is available from the British Library

Library of Congress Cataloging-in-Publication Data
Names: Adeyinka, Sarah, author. | Samyn, Sophie, author. |
   Zemni, Sami, author. | Derluyn, Ilse, author.
Title: Nigerian and Ghanaian women working in the Brussels
   red-light district / Sarah Adeyinka, Sophie Samyn, Sami Zemni,
   Ilse Derluyn.
Description: 1 Edition. | New York : Routledge, 2021. | Series:
   Routledge studies in development, mobilities and migration |
   Includes bibliographical references and index.
Identifiers: LCCN 2020048274 (print) | LCCN 2020048275 (ebook)
   | ISBN 9780367745530 (hardback)|ISBN 9781003158462 (ebook)
Subjects: LCSH: Prostitution–Belgium–Brussels. | Red-light
   districts–Belgium–Brussels. | Human trafficking–Nigeria. |
   Human trafficking–Ghana. | Nigerians–Belgium–Brussels–
   Social conditions. | Ghanaians–Belgium–Brussels–Social
   conditions. | Prostitutes–Belgium–Brussels–Social conditions. |
   Prostitution–Law and legislation–Belgium–Brussels.
Classification: LCC HQ207 .A45 2021 (print) | LCC HQ207
   (ebook) | DDC 306.7409493/32–dc23
LC record available at https://lccn.loc.gov/2020048274
LC ebook record available at https://lccn.loc.gov/2020048275

ISBN: 978-0-367-74553-0 (hbk)
ISBN: 978-0-367-74556-1 (pbk)
ISBN: 978-1-003-15846-2 (ebk)

Typeset in Times New Roman
by Taylor & Francis Books

Contents

Illustrations

Acknowledgements

We would like to express our profound gratitude to the Thematic and Territorial Support Service/Urban Prevention Programme, Municipality of Schaerbeek for commissioning and funding this project. We would also like to thank the guidance committee that held us accountable, asked critical questions, and gave us very helpful suggestions as we carried out the research; and without whom this project would have been impossible – M. Alain Vlaemynck and M. Johan Debuf (Brussels North Zonal Police – Human Trafficking Unit), Mme. Anne-Sophie Dutrieux (Pag-Asa), M. Bertrand Dhyuvetter (Coordination Unit of the Urban Prevention Programme), Mme. Émilie Haquin and Mme. Hélène Morvan (Thematic and territorial support service of the municipality of Schaerbeek), M. Franz Vandelook (Federal Police – Human Trafficking Unit), Mme. Isabelle Jaramillo (Espace P), M. Marc Weber and Mme. Alice Dobrynine (Representatives of the Mayor's office, Schaerbeek), M. Mehmet Bilge and Mme. Esma Cosgun (Alderman of Prevention and Head of Cabinet), Mme. Neila Jellouli (Schaerbeek Municipal Administrative Police Service), and Prof. dr. Gert Vermeulen (chair of the Department of Criminology, Criminal Law and Social Law, UGent). Thank you all very much for your critique, feedback, and consistent support.

We also wish to acknowledge the constructive contributions for the improvement of the first draft of this work made by Dr. Simon McMahon, Prof. dr. Ron Weitzer, Rik Samyn, Prof. dr. Michel Vandenbroeck, and Dr. An Verelst. Thank you.

Most importantly, we are extremely thankful to the women themselves who chose to be open and grant us insight into their working and/or living conditions. To you all, we extend our profound gratitude. As it is said in Nigeria: "we hail una o".

Glossary

Carré — one of the two types of places where window prostitution takes place in Brussels. A carré is part of a building on the ground floor used for prostitution. The person officially renting the place is the only one allowed to work there, and subletting is illegal. Although the space is commercially used, its intended legal use is residential.

Edo/Bini — an ethnic group in South-South Nigeria (one of the six geo-political zones of Nigeria) primarily originating from Edo State, which is one of the 36 states in the country. Benin City, its capital, is the main location where trafficking for sexual exploitation to Europe is organized and is recognized as one of the main human trafficking hubs in Africa.

Human Trafficking — (as defined by the Palermo protocol) "is the recruitment, transportation, transfer, harbouring or receipt of persons, by means of the threat or use of force or other forms of coercion, of abduction, of fraud, of deception, of the abuse of power or of a position of vulnerability or of the giving or receiving of payments or benefits to achieve the consent of a person having control over another person, for the purpose of exploitation" (UN, 2000).

Juju — refers to a type of belief, common in the spiritual belief systems of many West African countries including Nigeria, which is accompanied by a ritual. It comprises several elements including the conjuration of deities and the request that

	they intervene in human affairs. It is more commonly referred to as "voodoo" in the European context, and is often employed by Nigerian traffickers to ensure that the exploited women stay loyal to them – "their benefactors", and pay back the (extremely disproportionate) cost of their arduous journey abroad.
Madam	a female pimp, i.e. a woman who runs a house of prostitution, organizes the prostitution of others, or traffics women for the purpose of sexual exploitation.
Nigerian Pidgin	an English-based pidgin or creole language spoken as a "lingua franca" across Nigeria. Although it originates from and is closely linked to English, it is not intelligible for native English speakers.
Red-Light District	area where window prostitution takes place.
Saint-Josse-Ten-Noode	one of the 19 municipalities of the Brussels-Capital Region, often referred to as Saint-Josse. It is the smallest municipality of the Brussels Region in size and is located in the north.
Salon or bar	(for window prostitution) one of the two types of places where window prostitution takes place in Brussels. It is a building or part of a building with a front room in which one or more persons work in prostitution. Salons are categorized as commercial property and the work is organized in day and night shifts.
Schaerbeek	one of the 19 communes of the Brussels-Capital Region, located in the north-east. It is the second largest municipality in the Brussels Region in terms of population.
Twi	a dialect of the Akan language which is the most widely spoken language in Ghana.
Yemeshe	the practice of illegally subletting a carré in exchange for a percentage of the earnings. This generally means that the woman who works during the day sublets the carré during the night to another woman who then hands over up to 50 per cent of her earnings.
Yoruba	one of the three main ethnic groups in Nigeria.

1 An introduction to the ethnographic study of Nigerian and Ghanaian women working in Brussels' red-light district

1.1 Introduction

Two events in 2018 temporarily directed national attention towards the red-light district of the carrés behind Brussels North train station. First, the trial of the alleged "Mama Leather" was held, publicly exposing violent forms of exploitation and trafficking that were taking place in the area (*De Staandard*, 2018; *HLN*, 2018a). Second, a young Nigerian woman was murdered in front of her carré by an under-aged resident of the area (*HLN*, 2018b; *DeMorgen*, 2018). The events were overt signs of a degenerative situation and triggered questions about the safety of the women and the quality of life in the area. However, as one woman told us: "soldier go, soldier come, na barracks go remain", a popular saying in Nigeria meaning, "no matter what happens and how many changes occur, some things will remain the same, immovable and unchanging".

An estimated 150 African women stand behind the windows of the carrés today in an area that is characterized by outdated and neglected buildings, criminal activities (drugs, physical violence, trafficking, money laundering, etc.), nuisance (cars, noise, pollution), and the conflict between residential and commercial aspects of the neighbourhood (Brussels Hoofdstedelijk Gewest, 2015). While there is still a small presence of older (60+) French and Belgian women, the majority of the women working there are of Nigerian descent, a minority is of Ghanaian descent.

The new policy on prostitution of the municipality of Schaerbeek (2011) provides more assistance to the women and works towards their autonomy from pimps and human trafficking networks. This approach is said to have led to substantial improvements in the salons of the Aarschotstraat/rue d'Aerschot, the other red-light district nearby, but has failed to solve the grievances of the area of the carrés.[1] Actors "present" in the area (including social workers, the administrative police of the commune, and the local and federal police units) have expressed the difficulties they have in establishing trust relationships with the African women and in fully understanding what is going on. Next to cultural and linguistic barriers, the existence of institutional distrust often present in groups on the margins adds another layer of complexity. It is in this context that the Sub-Saharan[2] Women In Prostitution: Schaerbeek Ethnographic Research (SWIPSER) project came into being. It was commissioned and financed by the municipality of Schaerbeek and carried out by a Nigerian-Belgian research team (Sarah Adeyinka and Sophie Samyn) from Ghent University. The research was conducted between September 2018 and December 2019. A committee of several stakeholders met with the team regularly to provide insight and support to the researchers throughout the course of the project.

It is important to mention that this project was carried out within a limited time frame of one year as stipulated by the funders, which limited the time available for data collection and the amount of data collected and analysed. However, the importance of the research findings has already been demonstrated because the study enabled local actors to take steps in addressing some of the issues that we discovered and addressed. Also, we strongly believe that these findings have a global relevance, not only because the red-light district is embedded in a complex global web of inequality, migration, and sexualized racism that transcends the Brussels context, but also because of the movement of these women across borders and their work in prostitution in other European cities.

After the theoretical framework in the next paragraph, we take you through a short literature review of relevant themes on prostitution research. Thereafter, in Chapter 2 we explain the research design and data collection approach, with specific attention to the ethical considerations. Chapter 3 offers a historical contextualization of the area, focusing on legislation, the historical evolution of the red-light district of the carrés, Nigerian human trafficking networks, and the case of Ghanaian women. Chapter 4 presents our findings in four sections. The first three sections explore how the women navigate different realities: (1) the setting in which they work, (2) the migratory condition and the African community, and (3) the functioning of the red-light district of the carrés. They are based on the subjective accounts and heterogeneous experiences of the women and mirror the topics briefly discussed in the literature (prostitution and the city, prostitution, and migration and prostitution and policy). In the fourth section, four main challenges are identified. The conclusions in the last chapter lead to recommendations that may inform policy and practice working with these women.

None of this would have been possible without the very helpful input and feedback from the guidance committee and the various actors who set time aside to meet with us and support us.

1.2 Framework

1.2.1 Prostitution

Prostitution, or "the provision of sexual services for money or its equivalent" (Harcourt & Donovan, 2005, p. 201), is a contested subject and related policy is inevitably shaped by moral judgement (Munro & Della Giusta, 2008). Policies on prostitution vary worldwide, ranging from its criminalization to its decriminalization and even its regulation. Generally speaking, there are two juxtaposing approaches to the subject. On the one hand, there is the abolitionist perspective that equates all forms of prostitution with violence against women, considering it by nature as a criminal (or deviant) practice. On the other hand, the regulationist approach considers prostitution a legitimate form of labour (Showden, 2011). Belgium's federal legislation on prostitution states that soliciting and procuring clients is illegal, even if prostitution itself is legal; thereby limiting the extent of change that local policy makers can implement in its regulation, and allowing municipalities and their local police units to regulate prostitution in their respective tolerance zones (Boels, 2016; Loopmans et al., 2008; Vermeulen et al., 2007). The local government of Schaerbeek does not take sides in this debate; rather, it accepts the existence of prostitution on its territory and endeavours to eliminate nuisance and criminal activities associated with the activity (Brussels Hoofdstedelijk Gewest, 2015; Seinpost Adviesbureau, 2008; É. Haquin & H. Morvan, personal communication, October 18, 2018).

It is important to note that the authors do not take a moral stance in this debate nor feel the need to do so. Following authors like Peršak and Vermeulen (2014), Kantola and Squires (2004), Outshoorn (2005), Brooks-Gordon (2006), and O'Neill et al. (2009), this book was written on the premise that adapting one perspective would have led to a one-sided and biased analysis. Even within the research team, there was a difference of ideas on sex work and prostitution, which we believe enhanced our understanding of the complexities of the subject. We do not consider all prostitution as violence against women, neither do we consider it a job like any other. We simply aimed to understand the meaning of prostitution and sex work from the perspective of the participants of this research and mirror their experiences in this book.

1.2.2 Choice of terminology

In research, using the correct and appropriate language and terminology is extremely important as doing so helps to reduce unintended bias throughout the research process (Van Helsdingen & Lawley, 2012). Prostitution or sex work is not a neutral term and the phrases "women working in prostitution" and "women in prostitution" were intentionally used to describe the women and their job in their own words, to best capture their experiences without imposing ours.

The term "sex workers", though preferred by regulationists and deemed by some to be more neutral (Wagenaar et al., 2017), possesses a labour-rights connotation, which we only marginally encountered in the discourses of the participants. Most of the Nigerian and Ghanaian women in this study were ashamed of the work they did and hoped it would be temporary. Following Peršak and Vermeulen's argument, sex work "neglects the important stigmatizing aspect of prostitution" (2014, p. 16), which profoundly shapes the way it is practised and experienced. Thus, we preferred to use the term prostitution instead of sex work.[3]

Understanding and factoring in the Nigerian context influenced the researchers' choice of terminology because women who sell sex are referred to as "ashewo/ashawo" in Nigeria (Otutubikey Izugbara, 2005). The words "ashewo" and "ashawo" literally translated in the Yoruba language mean "money changer" and "money picker/gatherer". The terms may have been coined based on the premise that money exchanges hands between clients and women in prostitution. Importantly, a woman who is deemed as "loose" or "easy" is also referred to as an "ashewo"/"ashawo" (Chernoff, 2004; Okonkwo, 2010; Plambech, 2014). Ashawo is also a word in the Ghanaian language, Twi, that means "slut, prostitute, loose/easy" (Glosbe, 2020; Urban Dictionary, 2012). The term, therefore, carries the same stigma as does "prostitution".

It is therefore understandable that the women would refer to themselves as doing sex work, working in prostitution, and doing prostitution work but not as sex workers; thereby making prostitution and sex work an action that they take, rather than it being their identity (Plambech, 2014). The women referred to their job or the process of working in the red-light district of the carrés in these ways:

- "I dey do prostitution work" (I do prostitution work).
- "I dey do this work" (I do this job).
- "I dey work for this prostitution area" (I work in this area/field of prostitution).
- "I dey do ashawo/ashewo/sex work" (I do prostitution/sex work).

Labelling theory contends that minority groups and disadvantaged individuals and groups are more likely to experience labelling (Bernburg, 2009). Thus, it was important to the researchers that they referred to the women and their job in their own words, which is why we used the terms "women in prostitution" and "women working in prostitution".

1.2.3 Well-being and agency[4]

This project was commissioned by the municipality of Schaerbeek to inform policy, police, and other supportive services, hereby reflecting the political will to address the well-being and dignity of women working in the carrés. This research project is therefore situated within a perspective centred around human rights and human dignity as stated in the Universal Declaration of Human Rights (United Nations, 1948, art. 21.3).

First, it is important to begin by explaining why this is particularly relevant to women working in prostitution. Regardless of the moral stance, prostitution is regarded by all who are concerned as a high-risk activity (Kinnell, 2006; Peršak & Vermeulen, 2014; Sanders, 2004). In 2016, Amnesty International called attention to the numerous human rights violations that sex workers suffer worldwide. Potential risks include exposure to different forms of violence, malevolent exploitation, substance abuse, stigma, harassment from police and communities, and health-related issues (Hubbard & Sanders, 2003; Pitcher, 2006).

Second, in line with recent research that considers prostitution a "complex social and relational object" (Peršak & Vermeulen, 2014; Wagenaar et al., 2017), it is important to acknowledge the broader political and societal context that shapes the working conditions. Every red-light district has a distinct albeit constantly changing geographical and social fabric, which influences the well-being of the women working there.

While the concept of well-being risks being overused and becoming "void" of meaning, its holistic outlook is one of its key qualities (White, 2010). The concept of well-being does not assume objective categories with which to evaluate the lives of others (e.g. housing, health care, social network, etc.), but instead centres around what people value (Diener et al., 1997; Tiberius, 2014) and allows for diverging cultural perspectives, e.g. regarding individualistic and collective well-being (Suh et al., 1998). As such, well-being is simply understood as "doing well – feeling good" (White, 2010, p. 160).[5] We were interested in how the women were currently doing, therefore we did not dwell on past experiences (of their life back home or possibly their trafficked past) if they did not link their current challenges to past encounters, or bring them up themselves.

The decision not to probe into their past (regarding life back home or trafficking experiences) was taken by the researchers after the first few interviewees strongly declined to talk about it, saying that it is in the past and they would rather not discuss it. Whatever their reasons for declining may have been, they were entitled to do this and their decisions were respected. We were not seeking "trauma stories" (Brennan, 2005), but focused instead on what the women themselves considered as problematic or helpful.

Knowing how fast information (accurate or not) spread in the area, we decided to focus on the women's present and recent past experiences concerning their well-being. This prevented us from being labelled as people digging into their past, which could have led to more suspicion and made it more difficult to recruit participants. We witnessed the speed at which information is shared among the women when we walked into a room to introduce ourselves and the woman there said: "I know who you are, you are the researchers from Ghent doing research here." Therefore, to avoid the risk of being mis-labelled to our target group and others in the area, we adjusted our research questions to address the topic of our research and leave room for discussions about past experiences without expressly focusing on them.

When approaching the women, the Nigerian researcher mostly took the lead in initiating a conversation by introducing the researchers, asking where the women were from, and immediately switching to one of the local Nigerian or Ghanaian dialects, which seemed to put the women at ease. The researchers simply started interviews by asking in pidgin "how una dey now/how una dey do?", which loosely translated into English means "how are you doing/how are things with you?". As the conversation progressed on the women's terms, this allowed for the identification of beneficial aspects, as well as certain "difficulties", elements, or circumstances that threaten their well-being. It should be noted that the questions in pidgin English exude more depth and warmth than the English translation.

It is important to not dismiss the agency of the women in shaping and protecting their well-being (Maher et al., 2013; Peršak & Vermeulen, 2014; Vermeulen et al., 2007), with the underlying premise being that individuals are "active meaning-makers who are constantly in the process of constructing, reconstructing, and defending the meaning of their lived realities" (Elabor-Idemudia, 2003, p. 117). The women have developed valuable tactics and strategies (de Certeau, 1984) to deal with the challenges that they face in their work lives. These dynamics are important to recognize and include in our assessment to draft adequate policy recommendations that will genuinely protect their well-being. We also addressed them as experts of their own lives and asked them directly: "what changes would improve your work situation?" and "which policy suggestions do you have for this area?".

1.3 Literature

1.3.1 Prostitution and the city

Prostitution is often looked at in relation to where it takes place. This is especially the case in the urban context where women in prostitution are confronted with urban planning interventions, policing practices, and very often community resistance (Campbell & O'Neill, 2006; Sanders, 2005; Weitzer, 2014). Window and street prostitution are the most visible forms of commercial sexual exploitation and therefore incite the most attention (O'Neill et al., 2009).

Zones of window prostitution worldwide are referred to as "red-light districts", in reference to the neon lighting (Weitzer, 2014). Although the women remain indoors, they are visible from the street through the glass windows from where they attract clients. Weitzer (2014) distinguishes single-use zones that are mostly removed from the city core and only offer sexual services, and multi-use zones that also host other businesses and functions. Especially in the latter case, the societal perception or meaning of prostitution is very significant as the visibility of the windows makes the women observable not only to clients but also to all residents and passers-by and this situation makes the women more vulnerable to harassment (Gilfoyle, 1999; Campbell & O'Neill, 2006).

Although research tends to highlight prostitution as an urban phenomenon (Peršak & Vermeulen, 2014), recent trends of gentrification also include a moral dimension as contemporary criminalization and criminal policies focus on the exclusion of prostitution from public urban spaces (Peršak & Vermeulen, 2014, p. 15). Increasingly, prostitution takes place in private houses and brothels, facilitated by the abundance of advertisements through the Internet (Vandecandelaere, 2019). Meaning that although prostitution is often portrayed as being urban and here (in society) to stay, the exclusion of prostitution from the same urban spaces is often blatant.

1.3.2 Prostitution and migration

"Because the financial rewards of working in the commercial sex industry are comparatively high, increasing numbers of migrant women work in this industry in the UK and other European states" (O'Neill et al., 2009, p. 12). For many migrants, prostitution offers low-skilled and flexible work (with cash-based direct income) that pays more than domestic and cleaning work, which are the other sectors that historically attract migrant women (Agustín, 2006; Rodriguez, 2014). Migrants have been the dominant demographic in prostitution work in Europe since the 1970s with South-East Asian, Latin American, African, and Eastern European women (Kempadoo et al., 2012). Many of the challenges they face (linked to prostitution), such as little or no access to health care or vulnerability to labour exploitation, are interdependent and closely linked to their migratory condition (Sassen, 2003).

As migratory movements have changed, the diversity of sex markets has also increased and indicates the need for context-specific research (Andrijasevic, 2013). Thorbek and Pattanaik (2002) highlight the diversity in experiences when it comes to migrant prostitution, e.g. between permanent and temporary migrants. It is thus important to examine the specific migratory trajectories and conditions of the women and how these inform and shape their work in prostitution.

The literature on prostitution and migration is often intertwined with research on human trafficking as migrants from economically disadvantaged places are particularly vulnerable to being exploited (O'Neill et al., 2009). This is also the case for most of the Nigerian women who end up in prostitution (Carling, 2006). A significant number of these women came to Europe through the trafficking networks centred around Benin City and whose "modus operandi" has been extensively researched and documented since the 2000s (Carling, 2006; UNODC, 2006; Leman & Janssens, 2013; United States Department of State, 2018). Concerning policy, O'Neill et al. (2009) draw attention to the "conflict between a focus on the criminality of illegal migration and the need for a more humanitarian approach to trafficked persons" (p. 12).

1.3.3 Prostitution and policy

The complex relationship between migration, exploitation, and prostitution has always made it a difficult topic for policy makers (Wagenaar et al., 2017). Policies are often based on stereotypes and rarely pay attention to the experiences of the men and women involved. Furthermore, there are different opinions that inform and profoundly shape its legislation (Aronowitz, 2014). Ranging from complete criminalization to legalization, most countries employ a policy of tolerance and install certain regulations or practices to "monitor" the activity. Recent research has looked into the effects of different legislative models on the lives of women in prostitution (Campbell & O'Neill, 2006; Di Ronco, 2014; Peršak & Vermeulen, 2014) but the conclusions differ, often according to the ideological premise of the authors (Wagenaar et al., 2017). What is clear, however, is that the policies directly influence the well-being of those working in public forms of prostitution such as street and window prostitution. In some cases, policies have a reverse effect and can lead to violence or displacement of the activity (Wagenaar et al., 2017). That is why it is important to continuously examine the relationship between the intent and effect of policy while placing the well-being of the men/women at the centre. Finally, we should never lose sight of the way certain areas where prostitution takes place are being actively shaped by female sex workers (Hubbard & Sanders, 2003).

Since the 1980s, the number of support services aimed at men and women who work in the sex industry has increased. This initially happened within the framework of HIV prevention (Campbell & O'Neill, 2006). However, the focus broadened over the years and now actors providing support to sex workers work much more holistically to take into account the diversity of experiences (Pitcher, 2006). The importance of providing confidential and non-judgmental advice has been highlighted to be beneficial in monitoring exploitative situations. However, the "group" of men and women working in prostitution is very heterogeneous and research has shown that not all have the same needs or even want to access services (Pitcher, 2006).

Notes

1 Although this research was designed to describe the situation in Schaerbeek, the whole area of the carrés is considered, including the (largest) part located in Saint-Josse. The area is relatively small (three streets) and the municipal border is not visibly present. As a result, most of the women/ clients are not aware of this border.

2 The initial assignment of the research project drafted by the municipality of Schaerbeek used the term "Sub-Saharan women" to refer to the African migrant women in question. In this book, we will use "Nigerian and Ghanaian women" to refer to the two countries of origin of the participants, or occasionally "African women" which is more generally a label the women used when referring to themselves. It is however, important to note that for one of the participants the country of origin is unknown.

3 We use the term "sex workers" in this text when it is the term used by the author or organization that we are referring to.

4 "Agency" is the capacity of individuals to act independently and to make their own choices (Barker, 2003).

5 It joins three interrelated dimensions: a material dimension of a certain living standard, a subjective dimension of certain emotional aspirations, and, finally, a relational dimension. This relational aspect is very important, as well-being is also defined in relation to others or to one's place in society (White, 2010).

References

Agustín, L.M. (2006). The conundrum of women's agency: Migration and the sex industry. In R. Campbell & M. O'Neill (Eds.), *Sex Work Now* (pp. 116–140). Willan Publishing.

Amnesty International. (2016). Amnesty International policy on state obligations to respect, protect and fulfil the human rights of sex workers. https://www. nswp.org/sites/nswp.org/files/Policy%20on%20Sex%20Work%2C%20Amnesty %20International%20-%202016.PDF.

Andrijasevic, R. (2013). Migration and sex work, Europe. In I. Ness & P.S. Bellwood (Eds.), *Encyclopedia of Global Human Migration* (pp. 2740–2744). Cambridge University Press.

Aronowitz, A.A. (2014). To punish or not to punish: What works in the regulation of the prostitution market. In N. Peršak & G. Vermeulen (Eds.), *Reframing Prostitution: From Discourse to Description, from Moralisation to Normalisation?* (pp. 223–251). Maklu.

Barker, C. (2003). *Cultural Studies: Theory and Practice.* Sage.

Bernburg, J.G. (2009). Labeling theory. In M.D. Krohn, A.J. Lizotte, & G.P. Hall (Eds.), *Handbook on Crime and Deviance* (pp. 187–207). Springer. doi:443.webvpn.fjmu.edu.cn/10.1007/978-1-4419-0245-0_10.

Boels, D. (2016). Prostitutie en georganiseerde criminaliteit? De aanpak van wantoestanden binnen de sector. *Cahiers Politiestudies*, 39(2), 73–98.

Brennan, D. (2005). Methodological challenges in research with trafficked persons: Tales from the field. *International Migration*, 43, 35–54. doi:10.1111/j.0020-7985.2005.00311.x.

Brussels Hoofdstedelijk Gewest. (2015). Prostitutie. Studie uitgevoerd in 2013–2014 in het kader van de Brusselse Interministeriële Conferentie Sociaal-Gezondheid onder het voorzitterschap van de Minister-President van het Brussels Hoofdstedelijk Gewest. In N. Bailly, I. Thiry, J. François, M. De Gendt & M. Siaens (Eds.), *Brussels Observatorium voor Preventie en Veiligheid, Verslag 2015* (pp. 240–285).

Brooks-Gordon, B. (2006). *The Price of Sex: Prostitution, Policy and Society.* Willan Publishing.

Campbell, R., & O'Neill, M. (2006). Introduction. In R. Campbell & M. O'Neill (Eds.), *Sex Work Now* (pp. ix–xxi). Willan Publishing. doi:10.4324/9781843926771.

Carling, J. (2006). *Migration, Human Smuggling and Trafficking from Nigeria to Europe.* International Organization for Migration.

Chernoff, J.M. (2003). *Hustling Is Not Stealing: Stories of an African Bar Girl.* University of Chicago Press.

De Certeau, M. (1984). *The Practice of Everyday Life* (S. Rendall, Trans.). University of California Press.

DeMorgen. (2018, June 21). 17-jarige verdachte bekent moord op 23-jarige prostituee Eunice [17-year-old suspect confesses to murder of 23-year-old Nigerian prostitute Eunice]. https://www.demorgen.be/nieuws/17-jarige-verda chte-bekent-moord-op-23-jarige-nigeriaanse-prostituee-eunice~b9e0660d/.

De Standaard. (2018, May 31). Leden Nigeriaans prostitutienetwerk krijgen celstraffen tot 14 jaar [Members of the Nigerian prostitution network receive prison sentences of up to fourteen years]. https://www.standaard.be/cnt/dmf20180531_03538474.

Diener, E., Suh, E., & Oishi, S. (1997). Recent findings on subjective well-being. *Indian Journal of Clinical Psychology*, 24, 25–41.

Di Ronco, A. (2014). Regulating street prostitution as a public nuisance in the "culture of consumption": a comparative analysis between Birmingham, Brussels and Milan. In N. Peršak & G. Vermeulen (Eds.), *Reframing Prostitution: From Discourse to Description, from Moralisation to Normalisation?* (pp. 145–171). Maklu. http://hdl.handle.net/1854/LU-5652143.

Elabor-Idemudia, P. (2003). Race and gender analyses of trafficking: A case study of Nigeria. *Canadian Woman Studies*, 22(3), 116–123.

Gilfoyle, T.J. (1999). Prostitutes in history: From parables of pornography to metaphors of modernity. *The American Historical Review*, 104(1), 117–141. doi:10.2307/2650183.

Glosbe (2020). Definition of "ashawo". *Glosbe Twi-English dictionary.* https://glosbe.com/tw/en/ashawo.

Harcourt, C. & Donovan, B. (2005). The many faces of sex work. *Sexual Transmitted Infections*, 81, 201–206. doi:10.1136/sti.2004.012468.

HLN. (2018a, 31 May). Nigeriaans prostitutienetwerk "Mama Leather" betwist groot deel van feiten [Nigerian prostitution network: "Mama Leather" disputes many of the facts]. https://www.hln.be/nieuws/binnenland/nigeriaans-p rostitutienetwerk-mama-leather-betwist-groot-deel-van-feiten~a9cfe502.

HLN. (2018b, June 21). 17-jarige vast voor moord op prostituee [17-year-old jailed for murder of prostitute]. https://www.hln.be/de-krant/17-jarige-va st-voor-moord-op-prostituee~aa7cbcac/.

Hubbard, P., & Sanders, T. (2003). Making space for sex work: Female street prostitution and the production of urban space. *International Journal of Urban and Regional Research*, 27(1), 75–89. doi:10.1111/1468-2427.00432.

Kantola, J., & Squires, J. (2004). Discourses surrounding prostitution policies in the UK. *European Journal of Women's Studies*, 11(1), 77–101. doi:10.1177/1350506804039815.

Kempadoo, K., Sanghera, J., & Pattanaik, B. (2012). *Trafficking and Prostitution Reconsidered: New Perspectives on Migration, Sex Work, and Human Rights*. Routledge. doi:10.4324/9781315636269.

Kinnell, H. (2006). Murder made easy: the final solution to prostitution? In R. Campbell & M. O'Neill (Eds.), *Sex Work Now* (pp. 141–168). Willan Publishing. doi:10.1016/s0140-6736(01)76104-76101.

Leman, J., & Janssens, S. (2013). Creative adaptive criminal entrepreneurs from Africa and human trafficking in Belgium: Case studies of traffickers from Nigeria and Morocco. *International Journal of Criminology and Sociology*, 2, 153–162. doi:10.6000/1929-4409.2013.02.15.

Loopmans, M., Van den Hazel, R., & Van Oijen, S. (2008). Grensoverschrijdende prostitutie: beleid nodig met drie I's, Inzicht, Integraal en Internationaal. *Secondant*, 22(6), 26–29.

Maher, J., Pickering, S., & Gerard, A. (2013). *Sex Work: Labour, Mobility and Sexual Services*. Routledge. doi:10.4324/9780203101209.

Munro, V., & Della Giusta, M. (Eds.) (2008). *Demanding Sex: Critical Reflections on the Regulation of Prostitution*. Ashgate. doi:10.1007/s10657-010-9189-4.

Okonkwo, A.D. (2010). Gender and sexual risk-taking among selected Nigerian university students. *Sexuality & Culture*, 14(4), 270–305. doi:10.1007/s12119-010-9074-x.

O'Neill, M., Pitcher, J., & Sanders, T. (2009). *Prostitution: Sex work, Policy and Politics*. Sage Publications. doi:10.4135/9781446220726.

Onyeakagbu, A. (2020, May 6). 10 slangs only a Nigerian can understand. *Pulse NG* https://www.pulse.ng/lifestyle/food-travel/10-slangs-only-a-nigerian-can-understand/0kxhjg6.

Otutubikey Izugbara, C. (2005). "Ashawo suppose shine her eyes": Female sex workers and sex work risks in Nigeria. *Health, Risk & Society*, 7(2), 141–159. doi:10.1080/13698570500108685.

Outshoorn, J. (2005). The political debates on prostitution and trafficking of women. *Social Politics*, 12(1), 141–155.

Peršak, N., & Vermeulen, G. (2014). Faces and spaces of prostitution. In N. Peršak & G. Vermeulen (Eds.), *Reframing Prostitution: From Discourse to Description, from Moralisation to Normalisation?* (pp. 14–24). Maklu. doi:10.1080/13876988.2015.1013760.

Pitcher, J. (2006). Support Services for women working in the sex industry. In R. Campbell & M. O'Neill (Eds.), *Sex Work Now* (pp. 256–283). Willan Publishing. doi:10.1177/1057567707310564.

Plambech, S. (2014). Between "victims" and "criminals": Rescue, deportation, and everyday violence among Nigerian migrants. *Social Politics*, 21(3), 382–402. doi:10.1093/sp/jxu021.

Rodriguez Garcia, M. (2014). Prostitution in world cities (1600s–2000s). In N. Peršak & G. Vermeulen (Eds.), *Reframing Prostitution: From Discourse to*

Description, from Moralisation to Normalisation? (pp. 25–51). Maklu. doi:10.1080/13876988.2015.1013760.

Sanders, T. (2004). The risks of street prostitution: Punters, police and protesters. *Urban Studies*, 41(9), 1703–1717. doi:10.1080/0042098042000243110.

Sanders, T. (2005). *Sex Work: A Risky Business*. Willan Publishing. doi:10.4324/9781843926764.

Sassen, S. (2003, August 20). A universal harm: Making criminals of migrants. openDemocracy. https://www.opendemocracy.net/en/article_1444jsp/.

Seinpost Adviesbureau. (2008). Prostitutie Brussel in Beeld. https://adoc.pub/p rostitutie-brussel-in-beeld.html.

Showden, C.R. (2011). *Choices Women Make: Agency in Domestic Violence, Assisted Reproduction, and Sex Work*. University of Minnesota Press. doi:10.1080/1554477X.2013.805103.

Suh, E., Diener, E., Oishi, S., & Triandis, H.C. (1998). The shifting basis of life satisfaction judgments across cultures: Emotions versus norms. *Journal of Personality and Social Psychology*, 74(2), 482–493. doi:10.1037/0022-3514.74.2.482.

Thorbek, S., & Pattanaik, B. (2002). *Transnational Prostitution: Changing Patterns in Global Context*. Zed Books.

Tiberius, V. (2014). How theories of well-being can help us help. *Journal of Practical Ethics*, 2(2), 1–19.

United Nations. (1948). Universal declaration of human rights. https://www.un.org/en/universal-declaration-human-rights/.

United Nations Office on Drugs and Crime (UNODC). (2006). Measures to combat trafficking in human beings in Benin, Nigeria and Togo. https://www.unodc.org/documents/human-trafficking/ht_research_report_nigeria.pdf.

United States Department of State. (2018). Trafficking in Persons Report – Nigeria. https://www.refworld.org/docid/5b3e0ab6a.html.

Urban Dictionary. (2012). Ashawo definition, January 17, 2012. https://www.urbandictionary.com/define.php?term=ashawo.

Van Helsdingen, A., & Lawley, J. (2012). Modelling shared reality: Avoiding unintended influence in qualitative research. *Kwalon: Journal of the Netherlands Association for Qualitative Research*, 3, 1–7.

Vandecandelaere, H. (2019). *En vraag niet waarom. Sekswerk in België*. Epo.

Vermeulen, G., Moens, B., & De Busser, E. (2007). *Betaalseksrecht: naar regulering of legalisering van niet-problematische prostitutie?* Maklu.

Wagenaar, H., Amesberger, H., & Altink, S. (2017). *Designing Prostitution Policy: Intention and Reality in Regulating the Sex Trade*. Policy Press. doi:10.26530/oapen_627654.

Weitzer, R. (2014). Europe's legal red-light districts: Comparing different models and distilling best practices. In N. Peršak & G. Vermeulen (Eds.), *Reframing Prostitution; From Discourse to Description, From Moralisation to Normalisation?* (pp. 53–69). Maklu. doi:10.1080/13876988.2015.1013760.

White, S.C. (2010). Analysing wellbeing. A framework for development practice. *Development in Practice*, 20(2), 158–172. doi:10.1080/09614520903564199.

2 Research design of the ethnographic study on Nigerian and Ghanaian women working in Brussels' red-light district

2.1 Research aim

This project is a descriptive, ethnographic, qualitative study that attempts to gain a better understanding of the Nigerian and Ghanaian women working in the red-light district in Brussels while using ethnographic methods that focus on the experiences of the women. The women are considered experts of their own lives and all the data is based on their subjective experiences and interpretations. The research aims are:

1   To describe, through ethnographic fieldwork, the working experiences and interactions of Nigerian and Ghanaian women in prostitution in the red-light district of the carrés.
2   To identify the difficulties that the women face and understand how they deal with them.
3   To formulate recommendations towards the development of adequate interventions and policies for the well-being of the women.

This leads to subsequent research questions: How do Nigerian and Ghanaian women who work in prostitution experience the red-light district of the carrés? What are the difficulties they are faced with, and how do they manage them? Which changes could potentially be made to increase their well-being?

2.2 Methods

Data was collected using a multi-method qualitative approach, predominantly through ethnographic fieldwork that consists of detailed observations, informal interviews, and a focus group. In addition, these findings were enriched through interviews with stakeholders, document analyses, and interviews with two victims of human trafficking who hitherto worked in the area.

2.2.1 Ethnography

To understand certain social dynamics, it is fundamental to listen to the stories of their protagonists and observe society from their point of view. Using ethnographic methods, that "enable a process of representation of those who have often have little voice" (Sanders, 2004, p. 1707) prioritizes the perspective of the women. It demonstrates a willingness to include them in the policy-making process and affirms "the importance of the 'lived reality' (in all its diversity) of all those involved in sex work as a basis for theory, practice" (Campbell & O'Neill, 2006, p. x). Through foregrounding subjective experiences, qualitative research highly necessarily challenges theories on prostitution and migration that are ideologically and politically charged subjects.

> It is the face that adds individuality, distinguishes the individual from the mass, where she is only a number. Face separates, stands out, and prevents overgeneralization, which can only happen when one does not see the variance between individual experiences.
> (Peršak & Vermeulen, 2014, p. 14)

Finally, the informal and marginal quality of red-light districts requires an initially cautious attitude to find context-specific methods that work in a certain community. Ethnography offers scope for such a flexible and holistic approach, which is necessary to grasp the complexities, reveal unexpected truths, and defy pre-existing beliefs. Attributing a kind of "normality" to the field from the assumption that "prostitution is characterized by a variety of forms, working conditions and possibilities for agency, resistance, and negotiation" (Peršak & Vermeulen, 2014, p. 14), we listened to the experiences of the women. Examining how they navigate their particularly challenging surroundings helps us understand how the women give meaning to their environment and what informs their decision-making (Agustín, 2006; Campbell & O'Neill, 2006).

2.2.2 Stakeholder interviews

Between October 2018 and May 2019, semi-structured interviews were held with the following stakeholders/members of the advisory board to gather existing knowledge from those with on-the-ground experience: representatives from Espace P, the cell Administrative Police of Schaerbeek, PAG-ASA, the Local Police Brussels North (including the Human Trafficking unit), the Human Trafficking Section (Africa Unit) of the Federal Police, and those in charge of projects on prostitution and citizen participation – Schaerbeek Urban Prevention Programme.

2.2.3 Participants

The fieldwork was conducted in the red-light area of the carrés district between January and June 2019. The researchers started by spending time in the area to address key persons and explain the research. They distributed pamphlets which included their contact details and a brief explanation of the project. Both researchers were always together on the field and wore yellow vests with the university logo so that their role as researchers was clear. The fieldwork was done approximately twice a week, either during the day or in the evening.

Participants were mainly recruited based on their willingness to take part in the research and were addressed directly in their windows or, on a few occasions, in shops and bars in the area. Additionally, some women were recruited through snowball sampling, which in this case happened via referrals within the community. The researchers sometimes distributed condoms. These were always a welcome "gift", which sometimes incited conversations that we believe did not interfere with the neutrality of the researchers.[1] The use of Nigerian Pidgin, and on some occasions Yoruba and Twi, by a member of the research team was very significant in the process of establishing contact with the women, and it literally "opened doors". Finally, some events that took place in the carrés triggered participation, and the injustices which the women experienced during that period made them more open and willing to speak out. While the researchers met and introduced themselves to at least 70 women working in the area, a total of 38 women were interviewed, and Table 2.1 shows their profiles. This is important, as it reveals some of the diversity within the group.

Outside the field setting, interviews were conducted with two women who were recognized as victims of trafficking and were residents in a shelter of one of the relevant non-governmental organizations (NGOs). They had worked for eight months to two years in the red-light district of the carrés since 2017. During the interviews, they described their knowledge of the area without going explicitly into their personal stories or trafficking experiences.

Table 2.1 Profiles of 38 women interviewed

Country of origin		Work shift		Location of the carré		Age group[i]	
Ghana	8	Night	13	Schaerbeek	8	18–30 yrs old	15
Nigeria	29	Day	25	Saint-Josse	25	31–45 yrs old	11
Uncertain	1			Either/both	5	45+ yrs old	12

[i] This is the estimated age of the participants as we never asked the women for their exact age.

In the last phase of writing this book, we discussed the recommendations with some of the participants. Although their high mobility only made it possible to encounter less than half of the women whom the researchers knew and had interviewed, their feedback was very informative and led to the adjustment of some aspects of the recommendations.

2.2.4 Field notes

The data that was collected from the fieldwork resulted in comprehensive field notes of detailed observations and interviews. None of the interviews were recorded, and after the first few the process of taking field notes while on the field was discarded unless the curtains of the window were closed, and passers-by could not look in or see what was going on. The notes were written down by the researchers after each fieldwork session, which ensured that there were always two readings and perspectives on what happened or what was said on the field. The interviews were not recorded because the women who were already sceptical of the interview process would not have permitted them. The researchers also recognized that the process of taking notes during the interviews may have endangered the participants if they were seen by others "giving information", which the researchers then "wrote down". Thereby supporting the work of other researchers, who argue that recording an interview or taking notes mid-interview in places where passers-by can see and misconstrue what is going on, could cause participants to become uncomfortable thereby creating an unpleasant atmosphere (de Wildt, 2016; Cwikel & Hoban, 2005).

Interactions with the women mostly took place inside the carrés and were relatively concise and to the point, to avoid wasting valuable working time for the women. The researchers also paid attention to the women's non-verbals (some of which were cultural) and were able to recognize when to say or do certain things like end the interview or take a break. For example, there were instances when the researchers had to leave participants during the interview because a client either came in, or was lurking outside, and the woman's eyes kept looking in that direction. The women appreciated this sensitivity and respect for their time, and in those cases continued the interviews later on. The informal interviews and follow-up conversations were directed by a list of questions which were constantly adapted during the course of the research, and the exchanges ranged from short talks to more profound research–participant relationships (with many follow-up conversations). Some of the women kept in touch with the researchers outside the field through telephone conversations and messages.

Additionally, one focus group took place early in the morning with several women who worked at night and had just finished their shift. The group setting was useful for obtaining information about their feelings and opinions while working during the night shift, which the women all agreed was the most dangerous shift. It also revealed unexpected insights into the many differences between the women themselves.

While there, the researchers also came into contact with other individuals who frequented the area but did not belong to the target group (i.e. they did not work in prostitution in the area and/or were not of African descent). Rather, they were people conducting business in the area, residents, Belgian women in prostitution, etc. These encounters (14 of them) happened as a "by-product" that was often triggered by a curiosity about what the researchers were doing wandering around the area. They offered additional perspectives and further fuelled the understanding of the area, and in several cases, helped to secure access to the target group.

2.2.5 *Analysis*

All collected data were coded according to thematic analysis to identify recurrent themes, patterns, and structures in the dataset.[2] This inductive process of signification allowed us to stay as close to the women's words as possible. Additionally, through a process of triangulation (as a result of the multi-method approach of data collection) the experiences of the participants were held up against existing knowledge and general theories to increase the depth, quality, and scope of the results.

2.3 Ethical considerations

The project obtained the approval of the Ethical Committee of the Faculty of Psychology and Educational Sciences of Ghent University. The ethical protocol was created before the commencement of the fieldwork to ensure the quality and integrity of the research, and the well-being of the participants. Yet, the research process presented additional ethical challenges during the different stages of the research project (some of which are described above), which were dealt with through continuous reflection as a research team.

Obtaining the informed consent of participants ensured their voluntary participation and guaranteed that they were correctly informed. The participants were informed of what would happen with their data, the goal of the research, and their rights as participants – such as the right to withdraw participation at any time. Asking for written informed consent was not possible in this context as the women – through their position on the margin of society – are naturally suspicious of paper forms and signing documents. Instead, a verbal confirmation of consent which was approved by the ethical committee was requested (with both researchers as witnesses). After explaining the process to participants in a group such as this, verbal consent should suffice if they are worried about signing a document; after all, informed consent often offers more protection to researchers and their institutions than it does to the participants (Cwikel & Hoban, 2005; de Wildt, 2016; Kelly & Coy, 2016; McNutt et al., 2008). We also recognized that ethics goes beyond signed documentation and the fulfilment of the ethics committee's criteria, but rather is a continuous process of negotiation between the participants and researchers (Guillemin & Gillam, 2004; Samyn et al., 2020).

Since the fieldwork consisted of several informal moments with participants, the researchers always wore their UGent outfits so that their role as researchers was always evident. Aside from distributing condoms (and a small thank you gift at the end), none of the participants was remunerated to ensure that participation was voluntary. Some of the (younger) women whom the researchers encountered during the night shifts were being watched (by other Nigerian or Ghanaian African men or women) and did not want to be interviewed. To avoid endangering them, this was respected, and they were not pressured in any way to participate in the research.

Informed consent is at heart an interpersonal process between researcher and participant, where the prospective participant comes to an understanding of what the research project is about and what participation would involve and makes his or her own free decision about whether, and on what terms, to participate.

(Guillemin & Gillam, 2004, p. 272)

The researchers experienced tension with other roles in their relationships with the women, e.g. that of a practitioner (they both have prior experience in social work and counselling) or even that of a friend, making it sometimes challenging to merely observe. Subsequently, the research was accompanied by a process of constant reflection about interpretations and boundaries. We created a referral network of support services that we contacted beforehand, in case questions for certain types of support came up. The referral list was created in the belief that carrying out the interviews with the women without a reference point for assistance if needed would be unethical (Zimmerman & Watts, 2003). It consisted of organizations, and governmental and non-governmental agencies that offered assistance and care to groups that include (both documented and undocumented) women working in prostitution. This list was adapted during the course of the research as we discovered other organizations or realized that we had overlooked certain services which the women themselves reminded us of, thereby agreeing that "one way that some harm in a research context may be avoided (or at least mitigated) is providing respondents with information about services and support as part of the research protocol" (Surtees & Brunovskis, 2016, p. 140). We gave each of our participants a pamphlet with this referral network list at the end of the research and were able to refer some of the women to two of the organizations on the list.

A data management plan was drafted in compliance with the latest European legislation that ensures correct storage and usage of the data. Therefore, participants were encouraged to give us fake names, and our field notes were coded to protect any personal information. Nevertheless, the anonymization of the results is a complex process in the context of a geographically defined and known space. The "small population" problem has been discussed in relation to ethnographic studies, "which often focus on a particular village or town, where there is a high risk that individuals may recognize themselves in the talk of others" (Saunders et al., 2015, p. 619). Different techniques of pseudonymization, anonymization, and generalization were employed in this book to ensure the protection of the identity of the participants.

Finally, migration and prostitution are elusive phenomena that take place on the margins of society and are sometimes in violation of the law. Considering ethnography "a powerful tool for accessing women's lives" (Sanders, 2004, p. 1707), we must consider the public to whom the book is addressed and the risks of misinterpretation or misuse. Revealing secrets can have unwanted consequences, especially for people who have developed certain strategies of survival which they might prefer to keep hidden. It is for this reason that we went back into the field at a later stage to present our recommendations to the participants and to ask for their feedback.

2.4 Limitations of the study

The red-light district of the carrés, like any red-light district, is a complex field to research with its unique challenges. Therefore, certain limitations impacted the recruitment of participants and collection of data such as:

- *Limited time*: the interactions with participants took place during their working hours in their workplace, during the in-between moments, when the women were waiting for the arrival of clients. The fieldwork happened within a six-month period, which was the maximum time possible due to available funding and the expected deadline of the final report. Therefore, the amount of data that could be collected, and observation that could be done was limited.
- *No private space*: there were very few places in the area where the researchers could be without being in the way. Potential customers were always around, and the women did not want the research to interfere with their work. Even on the streets, the researchers had to pay attention to which street corner they stood at for some time as some of the women who did not have windows solicited clients on the streets. In one of the instances, the researchers were asked to move to another corner as they were (unknowingly) obstructing the woman working there. They quickly apologised and moved away. Therefore, visits to the area were often short and interviews were held inside the carrés.
- *The issue of trust*: the women are generally not trusting of out-siders (partly related to their background and current living con-text), which complicated access to the women and in-depth conversations, as a certain level of trust is essential in qualitative research. However, having a culturally and ethnically diverse team of researchers was of considerable added value and ensured a

necessarily culture-sensitive approach. The fact that one of the researchers is Nigerian incited a favourable level of curiosity because it also meant that the women could speak in their colloquial tongue and engage in small talk easily, often about topics related to Nigeria or life abroad as an African. This then made it possible to establish some level of trust in a very short amount of time.

- *Mobility*: there is a high turnover of women behind the windows. As a result of this, the researchers were unable to maintain contact with most of the women over longer periods. To address this issue, the researchers maximized the time they had with each participant during the interviews, with the knowledge that they may never see that participant again. This turned out to be the case for many of the participants; however, a few others stayed in touch.
- *Limited access to the women's private lives*: most of the women preferred to keep their private lives separate (this could be linked to the stigma associated with prostitution).

There is a widespread sense that prostitution simply cannot be taken seriously or ever achieve the status of other service occupations. Yet this folk wisdom is just that – a narrow, surface understanding that does not come close to recognizing the myriad dimensions of sex for sale, how it is experienced by workers and clients, and the value of considering policy alternatives "outside the box" of criminalization and marginalization.

(Weitzer, 2011, p. 3)

The researchers respected the women's wishes, thereby focusing purely on the interviews, conversations, and observations in the red-light district of the carrés. When they were invited into more intimate settings, like having lunch together or going out for dinner with a participant on a weekend, they accepted and did so at the request of the participants. All these elements resulted in a form of "volatile ethnography", which required a lot of flexibility and adaptation of the research method. Consistency in the researchers' visits to the field was one of the most crucial elements that helped to build credibility, as well as participating in some other economic activities in the area (the ordering/purchase of prepared meals, grocery shopping, and a hairdresser visit). Thus, observation became an important part of the data collection.

Some challenges impacted the researchers personally:

- The fieldwork had an emotional impact on the researchers linked to their being confronted with situations of deprivation and vulnerability and highlighted by seeing the neglect in the area as well as hearing the stories of violence that the women had experienced – some of which was very recent. In the same vein, however, the researchers were able to observe the resilience of the women through all this and they were often met with much hospitality, strength, and kindness, which was very humbling.
- The inability to reach some of the young women who seemed to be under the control of someone else. Most of these women worked at night and seemed extremely nervous when approached or kept looking at someone else (usually an older woman) for permission before responding to the researchers. This raised questions about their safety and care. But, after several conversations, the researchers decided to stay away from them to avoid jeopardizing their safety if they were under the control of a madam and seen talking with the researchers without permission. They were however given the researchers' contact cards and the research flyer and, through the course of the fieldwork, the researchers said hello to them whenever they walked by.
- The area is characterized by the presence of overt drug dealing, intoxicated persons, and petty crimes, and the researchers experienced feelings of insecurity at different times while on the field, including being followed. This highlighted, and helped the researchers to understand, the depth of insecurities that the women are faced with regularly. For safety reasons, the researchers had a security protocol in place which included, but was not limited to, informing the supervisors when on the field, leaving when there was any form of unrest in the area, and staying alert as a team. They also avoided going to the area in the middle of the night.
- The researchers' distinct backgrounds influenced their experiences in the field differently, especially with regards to safety and security in the area, accentuating the notion that perceptions of safety and security differ based on background and previous experiences of (in)security.

Two of the challenges highlighted by Shaver (2005) in research on the sexual service industry are the unknown size and boundaries of the population, and the stigma faced by those working in that industry, which may cause them to either refuse to participate or give cautious answers. These resonated within the study, as well as the number of women working there changing frequently and the stigma and discrimination that they face daily being a recurrent topic during the fieldwork.

Notes

1 At the end of the fieldwork, we gave them small thank you packs with condoms, hand sanitizer, intimate wipes, etc.
2 For analysis, MAXQDA was used: a software program designed specifically for computer-assisted qualitative and mixed methods data analysis.

References

Agustín, L.M. (2006). The conundrum of women's agency: Migration and the sex industry. In R. Campbell & M. O'Neill (Eds.), *Sex Work Now* (pp. 116–140). Willan Publishing. doi:10.4324/9781843926771.

Campbell, R., & O'Neill, M. (2006). Introduction. In R. Campbell & M. O'Neill (Eds.), *Sex Work Now* (pp. ix–xxi). Willan Publishing. doi:10.4324/9781843926771.

Cwikel, J., & Hoban, E. (2005). Contentious issues in research on trafficked women working in the sex industry: Study design, ethics, and methodology. *The Journal of Sex Research*, 42(4), 306–316. doi:10.1080/00224490509552286.

de Wildt, R. (2016). Ethnographic research on the sex industry: The ambivalence of ethical guidelines. In D. Siegel & R. de Wildt (Eds.), *Ethical Concerns in Research on Human Trafficking* (pp. 51–69). Springer International Publishing. doi:10.1007/978-3-319-21521-1_4.

Guillemin, M., & Gillam, L. (2004). Ethics, reflexivity and "ethically important moments" in research. *Qualitative Inquiry*, 10(2), 261–280. doi:10.1177/1077800403262360.

Kelly, L., & Coy, M. (2016). Ethics as process, ethics in practice: Researching the sex industry and trafficking. In D. Siegel & R. de Wildt (Eds.), *Ethical Concerns in Research on Human Trafficking* (pp. 33–50). Springer. doi:10.1007/978-3-319-21521-1_3.

McNutt, L., Waltermaurer, E., Bednarczyk, R.A., Carlson, B.E., Kotval, J., McCauley, J., et al. (2008). Are we misjudging how well informed consent forms are read? *Journal of Empirical Research on Human Research Ethics*, 3(1), 89–97. doi:10.1525/jer.2008.3.1.89.

Peršak, N., & Vermeulen, G. (2014). Faces and spaces of prostitution. In N. Peršak & G. Vermeulen (Eds.), *Reframing Prostitution: From Discourse to Description, from Moralisation to Normalisation?* (pp. 14–24). Maklu. doi:10.1080/13876988.2015.1013760.

Samyn, S., Adeyinka, S., Zemni, S., & Derluyn, I. (2020). Reflections on the interplay between procedural, relational and socio-political ethics in ethnographic research with West-African women working in prostitution in Brussels. *Qualitative Research Journal*, 20(3), 305–315. doi:10.1108/QRJ-02-2020-0009.

Sanders, T. (2004). The risks of street prostitution: Punters, police and protesters. *Urban Studies*, 41(9), 1703–1717. doi:10.1080/0042098042000243110.

Saunders, B., Kitzinger, J., & Kitzinger, C. (2015). Anonymising interview data: Challenges and compromise in practice. *Qualitative Research*, 15(5), 616–632. doi:10.1177/1468794114550439.

Shaver, F. (2005). Sex work research: Methodological and ethical challenges. *Journal of Interpersonal Violence*, 20, 296–319. doi:10.1177/0886260504274340.

Surtees, R., & Brunovskis, A. (2016). Doing no harm: Ethical challenges in research with trafficked persons. In D. Siegel & R. de Wildt (Eds.), *Ethical Concerns in Research on Human Trafficking* (pp. 137–154). Springer International Publishing. doi:443.webvpn.fjmu.edu.cn/10.1007/978-3-319-21521-1_9.

Weitzer, R. (2011). *Legalizing Prostitution: From Illicit Vice to Lawful Business*. New York University Press.

Zimmerman, C., & Watts, C. (2004). Risks and responsibilities: Guidelines for interviewing trafficked women. *Lancet*, 363(9408), 565. doi:10.1016/S0140-6736(04)15547-5.

3 Historical contextualization of the Brussels' red-light district where Nigerian and Ghanaian women work in prostitution

In this chapter, necessary background information is provided to better understand the broader context of the research setting. First, a short overview of Belgian legislation related to prostitution is provided. Second, we take a historical look at the red-light district of the carrés as a neighbourhood that has a long (and eventful) history of window prostitution. Third, we give a brief insight into the topic of Nigerian trafficking networks, which is too often misrepresented in the media. Finally, we look at the presence of Ghanaian women in the red-light district.

3.1 Prostitution legislation in Belgium

The activity of prostitution in Belgium as in most European countries finds itself in a legal twilight zone.[1] Before 1948, it was the responsibility of the municipalities to regulate prostitution on their territory. They organized mandatory registrations and medical checks (Vande Velde et al., 2007). In 1948, federal legislation took away this local mandate. While not prohibiting the activity of prostitution or paying for sexual services, from then on it became illegal to officially regulate the activity (Meheus, 1999).[2] The federal laws (with 1946 adjustments to Article 380) only oversee activities related to prostitution: (1) renting rooms for prostitution to realize an abnormal profit; (2) keeping a house of prostitution; (3) exploiting the prostitution of another; and (4) advertising prostitution have all been made punishable in Belgian Criminal law.[3] The criminalization of all third-party involvement has been criticized for having adverse effects on the sector (Vandecandelaere, 2019; Vermeulen, 2007).

In general, Belgium accepts the existence of prostitution in its territory and tolerates the forms of prostitution that are voluntary (Peršak & Vermeulen, 2014). On a municipal level, regulations can be made relating to public morality and tranquillity (through local urban planning and police regulations). In the private sector (escort, champagne bars, etc.), which expanded substantially with the rise of social media and the Internet, however, there is relatively little interference (Seinpost Adviesbureau, 2008).

For most of the second half of the twentieth century, local governments left a form of "unregulated tolerance" for public forms of prostitution, letting the sector regulate itself (Reinschmidt, 2016, p. 3). Since the 2000s however, municipalities began implementing more substantial local regulations[4] under the guise of "ensuring public order and tranquillity" in reaction to what was happening on their territories (Vandecandelaere, 2019). This was facilitated by the fact that they could now (from 1999) implement administrative sanctions (GAS fines) in addition to criminal sanctions that were slow and ineffective (Vandecandelaere, 2019). In consequence over the last 20 years, red-light districts in Belgium have profoundly changed: being relocated, restricted, or closed. Therefore, municipalities have taken very different approaches, influenced by the public response and political ideologies (Vandecandelaere, 2019).

On a national level, there are no indications that there is a political will to move towards a long-term vision regarding prostitution (Peršak & Vermeulen, 2014; Rodriguez Garcia, 2014). This has led to confusing situations in some parts of the country, most profoundly in Brussels.[5] Each of the 19 municipalities of the Brussels-Capital region has its local government, four of whom have to deal with forms of public prostitution on their territory, yet there is no joint approach (J. Debuf, personal communication, October 5, 2018). The red-light district of the carrés, which covers just three small streets, is located at the border of two municipalities that have very different approaches, making this a particularly complex case study.

3.2 Le quartier des carrés

3.2.1 How it began

Behind the North train station in Brussels, neon lights illuminate the windows on the ground floor where women sell sexual favours to men. Today we can clearly distinguish two red-light districts: (1) on Schaerbeek territory is the well-known Aarschotstraat/rue d'Aerschot, which runs parallel to the train tracks for about half a kilometre and (2) on the border with neighbouring Saint-Josse-ten-Node is the red-light district of the carrés, located on and around the Linnéstraat/rue

Linné and Plantenstraat/rue des Plantes. The first is home to commercial windows, referred to as salons or bars, where women predominantly of Eastern and Central European descent work in shifts,
while the red-light district of the carrés is located in a residential
area where only women who officially rent the property are allowed to
work. A few "older" (60+) Belgian and French women sit there
alongside a majority of Nigerian and Ghanaian women of all ages.
Although the name carré (French for square) comes from military
jargon and means "room or lodging" (É. Haquin, personal communication, January 7, 2020), it can also refer to the shape of the two
square rooms on the ground floor: the front room where the woman
solicits clients, and the back room where the sexual interactions take
place (Vandecandelaere, 2019). It is this area, locally referred to as
"Le quartier des carrés", that is of interest in this research.

  Although the current system of window prostitution is a relatively
recent phenomenon, the North quarter has attracted prostitution
activities in different forms since the nineteenth century, even before
the arrival of the North train station, when it was the home of
many small theatres (Vileyn & Difficile, 2018). After World War II,
prostitution allegedly spread to the territory of the municipality of
Saint-Josse-ten-Node, then the home of the first Italian immigrant
community who gradually left in the 1970s (Vandecandelaere, 2019).
Bernard Clerfayt, then mayor of Schaerbeek, explains in a news
article that the prostitution activity at that time was installed in
unnoticeable streets. The carrés on the ground floor looked like
apartments whose residents left the curtains open. With a bright
coloured light, the "residents" showed that they were waiting for customers. According to urban development planning, the carrés were
considered homes (Vileyn & Difficile, 2018).

  Clerfayt (Vileyn & Difficile, 2018) reveals here how the current legislative model of the carré can be understood historically. The streets
around the Linnéstraat/rue Linné and Plantenstraat/rue des Plantes
gradually turned into a red-light district within a residential neighbourhood. According to witness accounts, the area was occupied by
Belgian women, some French women, and a couple of African women
who worked autonomously in their carré (Vandecandelaere, 2019).
The women were familiar with the residents. They only worked
during the day and sometimes sent neighbourhood children on errands
(A. Vlaemynck, personal communication, October 5, 2018).

  Brussels is a city where the demand for commercial sex is very
high.[6] Apart from serving the "domestic" market, there is a link with
the mobile character of the city (Vandecandelaere, 2019) as tourism,

business, the presence of international institutions, and migration make Brussels the (temporary) home of many. In addition, in line with an abolitionist trend in some European countries, France has made prostitution illegal, criminalizing the purchase of sex and thus the clients. Therefore, so-called French sex-tourists more frequently cross their national border, also reaching Brussels' red-light district (J. Debuf, personal communication, October 5, 2018). However, as Vandecandelaere observed, women who work in red-light districts all over Belgium have been complaining about a decrease in clients over the past few years, which is probably a result of the substantial increase of other private forms of prostitution via the Internet (2019).

For a more theoretical discussion regarding the on-going debate on the position of the sex worker in Europe (in Belgium) and the controversies surrounding this, see Aronowitz (2014), Beran (2012), Gerassi (2015), and Jahnsen and Wagenaar (2019).

3.2.2 The arrival of African women

From the 1980s, within the context of broader migration flows into Europe, many migrant women coming from less privileged parts of the world entered the prostitution market in Brussels. Having limited options to earn a living, the lucrative aspect of prostitution was attractive, and as a result of their presence the prostitution market expanded and profoundly changed (Siegel, 2012). At first African women (of different nationalities) solicited clients in bars and went elsewhere to "work", and it was only in the 1990s that they entered the red-light district of the carrés (J. Debuf, personal communication, October 5, 2018). Some of the Belgian or French women retired and left their windows to them. The amount of carrés also increased considerably (Vandecandelaere, 2019).[7] Many of these women obtained citizenship through asylum procedures or marriage. With the tightening of immigration rules for non-Europeans in the 1990s, it became more difficult to travel legally or obtain legal residence documents, and African migrants became more vulnerable to exploitative situations (Olaniyi, 2011).

In this context of the expansion of prostitution activities in the late 1990s, many landlords sold their property to investors of Turkish origin who did not necessarily live in the area. Those investors, in turn, rented out the carrés to newly arrived immigrant women who agreed to pay a higher price (and this supposedly contributed to the retirement of Belgian prostitutes) (Vandecandelaere, 2019).

In May 1998, the carrés were attacked by (approximately 100) young men, breaking windows and throwing Molotov cocktails

(Brusselse Hoofdstedelijke Raad, 1998). This outburst of violence showed that relations between the women and the community were deteriorating, and several petitions asking for the suppression of prostitution were also circulated (Robert, 1998).[8] Whether or not this attack was racially motivated would require more research.

From the early 2000s, there has been an influx of women of Nigerian descent in the area and their arrival has challenged the traditional working model of the carré. Ignoring the "one woman per carré" principle, women now share spaces, sublet, pass on contracts, split rent payments, etc. (T. Tylova, personal communication, February 6, 2019). In addition, the African women working in the Aarschotstraat/ rue d'Aerschot, the other red-light district, gradually moved to the red-light district of the carrés (J. Hendriks & F. Vandelook, personal communication, November 10, 2018), thereby creating geographical segregation based on race and ethnicity. Of the women working in the carrés, more than 90 per cent are now of Nigerian or Ghanaian descent (personal communication stakeholders).

3.2.3 Local legislation

In 2011, the municipalities of Schaerbeek and Saint-Josse-ten-Noode collaborated to develop a joint policy to manage the red-light district of the carrés: (1) demarcation of the area, (2) new planning requirements, and (3) the application of the same fiscal policy. In Schaerbeek, this was part of a larger scheme to improve the conditions for window prostitution on its territory, mostly aimed at the red-light district in the Aarschotstraat/rue d'Aerschot.[9]

The new Urban Planning and Police Regulations were based on the "Antwerp-model",[10] set up to avoid the expansion of the tolerated zone and to minimize nuisance and criminality. They introduced a compulsory "certificate of conformity" with three main conditions: (1) the carrés must comply with certain material requirements (imposing minimum conditions on the surface, sanitation, electrical and water installations, fire safety, etc.); (2) the women are obligated to register with the administrative police, which requires them to be legal residents with work permits; and (3) one address can be linked to only one certificate so that no more than one woman can work in the same carré, and the police can easily verify compliance.

While the transition to the new regulations in Schaerbeek began in 2013, and they have been mostly implemented, the initial focus was primarily on the red-light district in the Aarschotstraat/rue d'Aerschot, where most of the salons were in unsanitary conditions constituting a major source of nuisance for the inhabitants (É. Haquin, personal communication, October 18, 2018). The administration of neighbouring Saint-Josse, however, abandoned the approach in 2012 and the current local authorities are looking at ways to end prostitution in their municipality. Some of these attempts have been met with resistance from sex workers and contradict legislation that falls outside the jurisdiction of the municipality.[11] This results today in a red-light district that is neglected and self-regulated (personal communication stakeholders; Vandecandelaere, 2019).

3.3 Nigerian human trafficking networks

In the context of global migration flows in the 1980s and 1990s, a vast diaspora of Nigerians was formed predominantly in the United States, the UK, and Italy, but also in countries like the Netherlands, Ireland, Germany, and Belgium (Zibouh & Martiniello, 2015). The Edo people, an ethnic group in the South-South of Nigeria, mostly settled in Italy where both men and women came to work in tomato fields, to trade in textiles and jewellery, and as Christian pilgrims on tourist visas (Ellis, 2016). Scholars agree that it was during those years that some Edo women discovered the lucrative activity of prostitution, thereby sharing the market with other migrant women (Olaniyi, 2011).

In the 1990s, Europe introduced stricter migration policies and it generally became more expensive to travel, which then created the debt or loan system in the migratory context. Some of the first-generation Edo migrants in Italy became the first madams or sponsors bringing girls over to work in prostitution. Born out of the benign gesture of facilitating the journey for relatives by advancing the money, it increasingly turned into a lucrative and exploitative business, generating huge profits (Simoni, 2013). The first madams soon controlled entry into the business, keeping it in the hands of Edo women.

The modus operandi of the networks is well known and has continued to develop with only minor changes (Carling, 2006; Okojie et al., 2003; Osakue, 1997; Plambech, 2017; Samyn, 2018). Women, mostly aged between 15 and 25, are recruited by a relative or acquaintance of the family who works for a madam in Europe. Before leaving, the woman/girl undergoes a juju ritual in which she promises to pay back her debt (= travel expenses with interest) and remain loyal to her benefactor. She is then accompanied to Europe by men (also called trolleys), who arrange the travel.[12] This may be overland (through Libya or Morocco) or by air (using false or no documents). Once in Europe, the woman usually meets her madam and is set up to work in prostitution until she has finished repaying her debt.

The lucrative aspect of the phenomenon has economically and socially changed many communities in Edo state. Once the networks, infrastructures, and expectations were established, the migration flow was reinforced, and despite anti-trafficking operations, it has continued to grow (Plambech, 2017; Samyn, 2018). Apart from the financial gains for the sponsors, other economies have appeared that profit from the movement of these women, through remittances for families, the smuggling trade, the rescue sector (related to human trafficking), and the detention and repatriation of migrants (see Plambech, 2017). Additionally, traditional and evangelist priests, immigration officers, and lawyers have been known to profit from the business (United States Department of State, 2018).

We must mention the prominent role that Nigerian madams play in the exploitation of Nigerian women and how they keep the cycle of exploitation going. Most of these women were themselves formerly sex workers and now put other women through the same experiences that they had, thereby blurring the line between victim and offender and portraying how the global economy is structured to ensure the replication of exploitation (Olaniyi, 2003; Siegel & de Blank, 2010).

In 2018, the King of Benin (Oba of Benin) made a public declaration against traffickers who bring Bini women to Europe for prostitution and broke the curses that were placed on the women through juju rituals (Ibileke, 2018). While this is a welcome development in the fight against exploitation and human trafficking, not all trafficked Nigerian women are from Benin, and most of the participants in this research had been in Europe for at least five years, during which some had already repaid their debts. This raises questions about what other strategies are being used by the traffickers and how the King's declaration was perceived and interpreted by trafficked, non-Bini women.

Since the mid-1990s Belgium has developed tools and expertise designed to fight human trafficking networks and to protect the victims: new legislation,[13] police efforts, and shelters. In 1994 Team Afrika was set up within the Gendarmerie of the Belgian police, a team that exclusively investigates Nigerian prostitution networks, which was later integrated into the Federal Judicial Police. It came as a response to the observed and steadily growing presence of young Nigerian women in prostitution in Brussels (J. Hendriks & F.

Vandelook, personal communication, November 10, 2018). Although Team Afrika has investigated cases across Belgium over the years,[14] the red-light district of the carrés in Brussels has remained a constant setting of scrutiny, and the human trafficking section of the local police (PolBruNo) collaborates with the Federal unit to detect possible victims.

3.4 Ghanaian women in the carrés

It is important to highlight the under-researched group of Ghanaian women working in prostitution in Brussels. During the course of this research, it was apparent that while some Ghanaian women worked in the carrés, very little was known about them, of their stance on prostitution legislation in Belgium, and their well-being and concerns. They were all older women (50+) who had resided in Belgium for decades and worked in the red-light district for most of that time.

Ghanaian women have been known to emigrate to work in prostitution, e.g. in Abidjan in Ivory Coast, which means being away from their families (Anarfi, 1998). The women work for themselves while supporting their families that stay behind (Tylova, 2014). In the interviews with stakeholders, Ghanaian women working in the carrés were mentioned as having been present in the red-light district for a long time, with some of them allegedly being involved in the exploitation happening there. This shows a major gap in knowledge about Ghanaian women here, as stakeholders estimate that they represent approximately 18–25 per cent of the African women working in the carrés.

According to Tylova (2014), Ghanaian women entered Europe, probably in the 1960s and 1970s, mainly via Italy (later via Spain or Greece) where it is easier to obtain residence permits. As in Africa, Tylova continues, Ghanaian women mainly work independently. Some of them have settled in Belgium hoping to save money to invest in real estate or business in Ghana, for their families and for the day they will return to their home country (Kempadoo & Doezema, 1998).

A large proportion of the existing literature regarding prostitution and African women in Europe, except for the works of researchers such as Altink (1996), Adomoko-Ampofo (1997), and Siegel and de Blank (2010), is solely focused on Nigerian women. Whether this is as a result of their presence in Europe being unique to Belgium and the Netherlands or whether this is just under-researched is yet to be known.

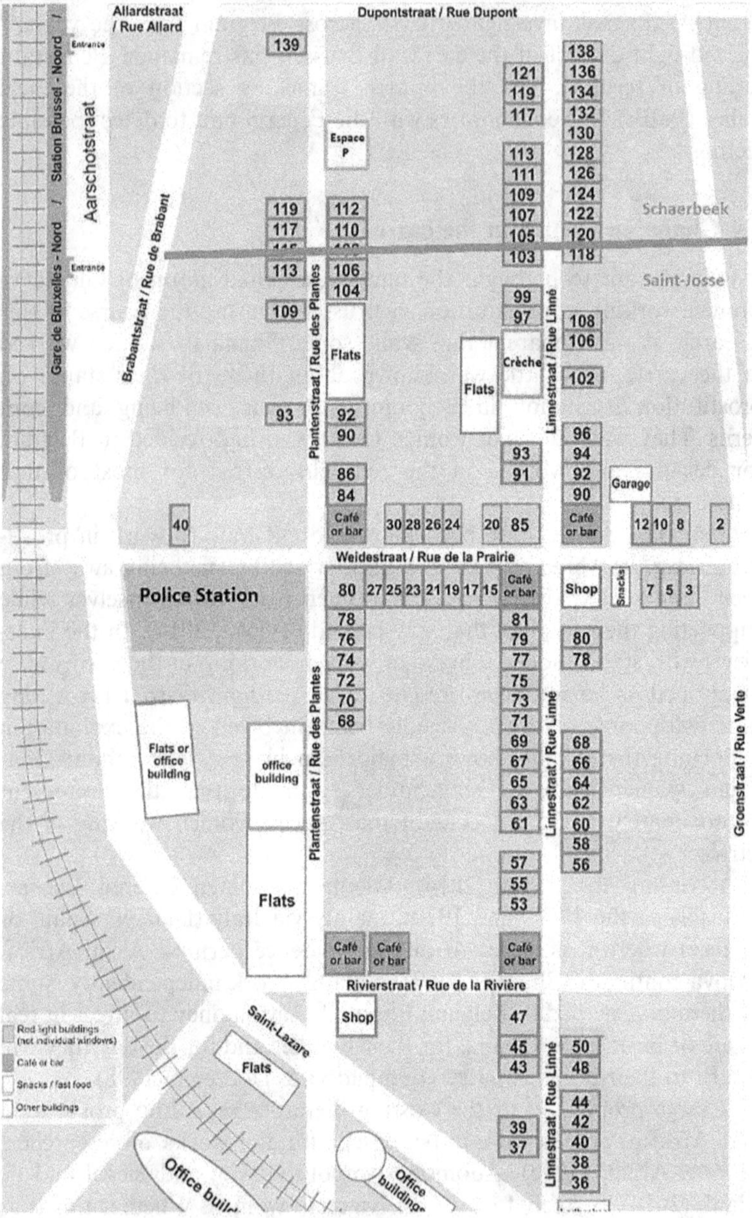

Figure 3.1 Map of the Brussels red-light district carrés, 2019

Notes

1 The legality of prostitution in Europe varies by country.
2 Belgium adheres to the 1950 New York convention for the suppression of the traffic in persons and of the exploitation of the prostitution of others.
3 See Criminal Code article 380, § 1. In a move towards decriminalization, points 1 to 4 were omitted in a proposal of Minister Geens just before the fall of the government of Michel I in 2018. It is very unclear if the newly elected government will advance in this way.
4 These are sometimes in violation of federal law, especially regarding laws on privacy (Vandecandelaere, 2019).
5 In some cases, it has merely benign consequences. In the Kortrijksesteenweg (aka *Chaussée d'amour* because of the presence of many brothels), one of the brothels stands out because of its ostentatious lighting. It is unnoticeably located in a municipality different from the others which does not have restrictive laws regarding the exterior of the establishments.
6 Stakeholders suspect that there is a high demand for commercial sex in Brussels. "A 2017 sensitizing campaign against trafficking by the Samilia foundation confirmed this when they posted a fake ad with a telephone number in public places in European cities and registered the number of calls. Brussels came out on top" (J. Debuf, personal communication, October 5, 2018).
7 The number of carrés went from 83 in 1993 to 107 in 2001 in Saint-Josse. In Schaerbeek it fluctuates around 30.
8 At that time, there were also two peepshows in the area, and street prostitution (of Latina women and transgenders) took place (Vandecandelaere, 2019).
9 E.g. they implemented lower standards of hygiene for the carrés because they feared that in that area it was likely the women would have to make the adjustments themselves instead of the house owners doing it (É. Haquin, personal communication, January 7, 2020).
10 The Antwerp model: in 1999 Antwerp launched a new and integrated policy on window prostitution that has continued to exist until today. In Belgium this area of public prostitution is considered an example of a successful red-light district (see Vandecandelaere, 2019; Weitzer, 2014).
11 The last two police regulations of Saint-Josse were challenged in the Council of State who ruled in favour of the sex workers and annulled the regulations.
12 This phenomenon too has changed over time and they are not necessarily accompanied by men anymore.
13 See https://www.payoke.be/about-us/legislation/.
14 Between 1994 and 2019, they discovered 18 Nigerian trafficking networks with a total of 266 victims and 182 suspects (J. Hendriks & F. Vandelook, personal communication, November 10, 2018).

References

Adomoko-Ampofo, A. (1997). *To Be or Not to Be a Prostitute: The Example of Ghanaian Prostitutes in Netherlands*. Institute of African Studies, University of Ghana.

Altink, S. (1996). *Stolen Lives: Trading Women into Sex and Slavery.* Routledge. doi:10.4324/9780203708132.

Anarfi, J.K. (1998). Ghanaian women and prostitution in Cote d'Ivoire. In K. Kempadoo & J. Doezema (Eds.), *Global Sex Workers* (pp. 104–113). Routledge.

Aronowitz, A.A. (2014). To punish or not to punish: What works in the regulation of the prostitution market. In N. Peršak & G. Vermeulen (Eds.), *Reframing Prostitution: From Discourse to Description, from Moralisation to Normalisation?* (pp. 223–251). Maklu. doi:10.1080/13876988.2015.1013760.

Beran, K. (2012). Revisiting the prostitution debate: Uniting liberal and radical feminism in pursuit of policy reform. *Law & Inequality: A Journal of Theory and Practice*, 30(1), 19–56.

Brusselse Hoofdstedelijke Raad. (1998). Bulletin van de interpellaties en mondelinge en dringende vragen. Vergadering van donderdag 28 mei 1998. http://www.weblex.irisnet.be/data/crb/biq/1997-98/00034/N/images.pdf.

Carling, J. (2006). *Migration, Human Smuggling and Trafficking from Nigeria to Europe.* International Organization for Migration.

Ellis, S. (2016). *This Present Darkness: A History of Nigerian Organized Crime.* Oxford University Press. doi:10.3917/afco.259.0171.

Gerassi, L. (2015). A heated debate: Theoretical perspectives of sexual exploitation and sex work. *Journal of Sociology and Social Welfare*, 42(4), 79–100.

Ibileke, J. (2018, March 9). Human trafficking: Oba places curses on offenders, collaborating sorcerers, cultists. *The News Nigeria.* https://www.thenewsnigeria.com.ng/2018/03/09/human-trafficking-oba-places-curses%E2%80%8B-on-offenders-collaborating-sorcerers-cultists/.

Jahnsen, S.Ø., & Wagenaar, H. (Eds.) (2019). *Assessing Prostitution Policies in Europe.* Routledge. doi:10.4324/9781138400238.

Kempadoo, K., & Doezema, J. (Eds.) (1998). *Global Sex Workers.* Routledge.

Meheus, A. (1999). *Van opjaagbeleid tot gedoogbeleid: de aanpak van prostitutie in Nederland en Vlaanderen doorgelicht.* Maklu.

Okojie, C.E.E., Okojie, O., Eghafona, K.A., Vincent-Osaghae, G., & Kalu, V. (2003). *Report of Field Survey in Edo State, Nigeria. Program of Action Against Trafficking in Minors and Young Women from Nigeria into Italy for the Purpose of Sexual Exploitation.* The United Nations Interregional Crime and Justice Research Institute.

Olaniyi, R. (2003). No way out: The trafficking of women in Nigeria. *Agenda: Empowering Women for Gender Equity*, 55, 45–52.

Olaniyi, R. (2011). Global sex trade and women trafficking in Nigeria. *Journal of Global Initiatives: Policy, Pedagogy, Perspective*, 6(11), 111–131.

Osakue, G. (1997). Exposing age-old problems: Trafficking in women in Nigeria. *Women's World*, 32, 25–27.

Peršak, N., & Vermeulen, G. (2014). Faces and spaces of prostitution. In N. Peršak & G. Vermeulen (Eds.), *Reframing Prostitution: From Discourse to*

Description, from Moralisation to Normalisation? (pp. 14–24). Maklu. doi:10.1080/13876988.2015.1013760.

Plambech, S. (2017). Sex, deportation and rescue: Economies of migration among Nigerian sex workers. *Feminist Economics,* 23(3), 134–159. doi:10.1080/13545701.2016.1181272.

Reinschmidt, L. (2016). Prostitution in Belgium: Federal legislation and regulation at the local level. Observatory for Sociopolitical Developments in Europe. https://www.beobachtungsstelle-gesellschaftspolitik.de/f/18c8191 7c6.pdf.

Robert, F. (1998, May 18). La petite commune de Saint-Josse compte ses vitres brisées et s'attend à une nouvelle flambée de violence Bruxelles. *Le Soir.* https://www.lesoir.be/art/la-petite-commune-de-saint-josse-compte-ses-vitres_t-19980518-Z0F8E9.html.

Rodriguez Garcia, M. (2014). Prostitution in world cities (1600s–2000s). In N. Peršak & G. Vermeulen (Eds.), *Reframing Prostitution: From Discourse to Description, from Moralisation to Normalisation?* (pp. 25–51). Maklu. doi:10.1080/13876988.2015.1013760.

Samyn, S. (2018). Indentured sex work migration from Edo state to Europe: Navigation in violent contexts [unpublished master's thesis]. Ghent University.

Seinpost Adviesbureau. (2008). Prostitutie Brussel in Beeld. https://adoc.pub/p rostitutie-brussel-in-beeld.html.

Siegel, D. (2012). Mobility of sex workers in European cities. *European Journal on Criminal Policy and Research*, 18(3), 255–268.

Siegel, D., & de Blank, S. (2010). Women who traffic women: The role of women in human trafficking networks – Dutch cases. *Global Crime*, 11(4), 436–447. doi:10.1080/17440572.2010.519528.

Simoni, V. (2013). I swear an oath. Serments d'allégeances, coercitions et stratégies migratoires chez les femmes nigérianes de Benin City. In B. Lavaud-Legendre (Ed.), *Prostitution nigériane: entre rêves de migration et réalités de la traite* (pp. 33–60). Karthala.

Tylova, T. (2014). La construction de l'identité sociale des personnes prostituées d'origine africaine à Bruxelles [unpublished master's thesis]. Université libre de Bruxelles.

United States Department of State. (2018). Trafficking in Persons Report – Nigeria. https://www.refworld.org/docid/5b3e0ab6a.html.

Vande Velde, L., De Vrieze, S., & De Proost, S. (2007). Prostitutiebeleid in Antwerpen, Brussel en Charleroi. In G. Vermeulen (Ed.), *Betaalseks: naar regulering of legalisering van niet-problematische prostitutie?* (pp. 309–357). Maklu.

Vandecandelaere, H. (2019). *En vraag niet waarom. Sekswerk in België.* Epo.

Vermeulen, G. (2007). European quality labels in prostitution as an illegal sector. In G. Vermeulen (Ed.), *EU Quality Standards in Support of the Fight against Trafficking in Human Beings and Sexual Exploitation of Children* (pp. 274–278). Maklu.

Vileyn, D., & Difficile, L. (2018, November 8). Jouw vraag. Sinds Wanneer is er prostitutie in de Aarschotstraat? *Bruzz*. https://www.bruzz.be/videoreeks/don derdag-8-november-2018/video-jouw-vraag-sinds-wanneer-er-prostitutie-de.

Weitzer, R. (2014). Europe's legal red-light districts: Comparing different models and distilling best practices. In N. Peršak, & G. Vermeulen (Eds.), *Reframing Prostitution; From Discourse to Description, from Moralisation to Normalisation?* (pp. 53–69). Maklo. doi:10.1080/13876988.2015.1013760.

Zibouh, F., & Martiniello, M. (2015). The migration of Nigerian Women to Belgium. In C. Timmerman, M. Martiniello, A. Rea, & J. Wets (Eds.), *New Dynamics in Female Migration and Integration* (pp. 185–206). Routledge. doi:10.4324/9781315885780.

4 Findings of the ethnographic study on Nigerian and Ghanaian women working in Brussels' red-light district

This fourth chapter presents the findings that result from an analysis of the fieldwork. Looking at prostitution as a relational object determined by the political, societal, and geographical context in which it takes place (Peršak & Vermeulen, 2014), we will examine the experiences of the women concerning (4.1) the setting, (4.2) the migratory condition and the diasporic community, and (4.3) the functioning of the red-light district of the carrés. In the final section (4.4), we identify four challenges that emerged from these findings and that put the well-being of the women at risk. The text is enriched with numerous excerpts from the field notes of the researchers. Occasionally, we refer to literature that confirms or contradict the findings or offers an explanation for observations that were made. In this way, we try to create a dialogue between this case study and existing theories and knowledge on prostitution.

4.1 Prostitution and the city: the setting

"You have to see this. Look at this video! It was so scary. Really. Do you see?" A few months into the fieldwork and we are in one of the bars in the area, sitting at a table with a few of the women. We look at the phone Edith passed to us. It showed what took place on New Year's Eve. Young men, who have their faces covered by masks, are on the street. There is smoke everywhere and people shouting. Didi tells us the men came to intimidate them. They burnt garbage, broke windows of carrés, turned over a car ... The women hid inside bars and houses. The police arrived but didn't intervene and after things calmed down there was never any political reaction. Just six months after the women went into the street asking for protection, following the murder of Eunice,[1] it seems nothing had changed.

(field notes, April 2019)[2]

This unsettling account is illustrative of the many problems in the red-light district of the carrés. This section will focus on the relationship between the women and their direct surroundings: how do they move in this unsettling space? How do they interpret it? And finally, how do they deal with it?

4.1.1 Demographic context

After Dubai, Brussels is the city with the highest percentage of residents of foreign origin (International Organization for Migration, 2015), and it is a city of contradictions and inequality. While it is a city of diplomats and lobbyists, 30 per cent of its inhabitants live below the poverty line (Observatorium voor Gezondheid en Welzijn van Brussel Hoofdstad, 2015). The North quarter in which the red-light district is located, considering its proximity to the North train station, has always been a place of "passage" and is characterized by important population movements. It is both a space where newly arrived migrants settle permanently, as well as a transit hub for migrants en route to other European cities (Di Ronco, 2014; Gsir, 2017). Here, ethnic differences are translated into socio-economic differences, and the average income in the North Quarter is lower than the regional average (Observatorium voor Gezondheid en Welzijn van Brussel Hoofdstad, 2015). The population is further characterized by very young inhabitants with a high percentage of young single people, large families, and a predominantly male public representation (Renovas, n.d.). The North quarter also attracts many "visitors" as the stores on Brabantstraat/rue de Brabant offer an impressive array of products from all over the world: food, furniture, herbs, clothing, shoes, etc., which are hard to find elsewhere. Higher up on the border between Saint-Josse and Schaerbeek is another important commercial axis: "Little Anatolia". This stretch of the Haachtsesteenweg/chaussée de Haecht is characterized by a strong ethnic identity, namely that of the Turkish community (Renovas, n.d.).

> "We are in Arab land here!"
>
> (Lucy, field notes, May 2019)

The women often use "Arab" interchangeably with "Moroccan" to refer to other (non-black) persons with migrant backgrounds, mostly of Turkish or Moroccan descent.[3] In addition, the terms are also associated with a Muslim identity or the fact that a person speaks what they understand to be Arabic. "Moroccans" are also considered different from "Belgians", whom the women refer to as "white".

Cheap rent, especially in the apartments in the red-light district of the carrés, has attracted many newly arrived migrants, and, most recently, families from Eastern European countries (É. Haquin & H. Morvan, personal communication, October 18, 2018). The vacancy rate is high (IBSA, 2016a; IBSA, 2016b), which leads to situations of precarity, as is illustrated by the next field note.

Today we witness an eviction in the area. A woman, of Roma migration background, is standing outside on the street with her small son. She is crying. A locksmith is busy changing the locks. "They put me and my baby outside," she tells us. "We were squatting in one of the apartments. Now we have nowhere else to go."

(field notes, May 2019)

Finally, the prostitution activities, drug dealing, and bars attract outsiders to the area both night and day, ranging from innocent shoppers to "disorderly individuals" (Weitzer, 2014, p. 59).

"There is a lack of social cohesion and people blame each other for the state of things," several of the stakeholders explained (personal communication). In contexts of deprivation, individuals tend to show favouritism towards their own "group" and may react negatively towards outsiders. This is a situation that can lead to prejudice and discrimination (Turner, 1975) and something we observed in the area.

"The children play football on the street. What kind of behaviour is this? This is not a park. They should play in the park. It's no place to be playing here. The ball can break a window."

(Nancy, field notes, May 2019)

Although the older women often speak some French, most of the African women in this area speak English or Nigerian Pidgin (next to their mother tongue of Edo, Yoruba, etc. and other acquired languages like Italian or Spanish). They speak other European languages because, for the majority of them, Italy, France, or Spain was their country of arrival and residence in Europe for many years before coming to Belgium; and they often refer to those countries as "home". Most of the residents of the area of the carrés, however, speak French, Turkish, Arabic, or other languages. Furthermore, moral opinions regarding drugs, alcohol, and prostitution sometimes complicate interactions more than language and cultural barriers.

4.1.2 Structural neglect of the area and its people

> Diamond says she misses Italy, while she looks up at the ceiling, where paint is peeling off and water stains leave discoloured patches. "Look at the state of the buildings. Brussels is old and dirty. Also, the apartment where I live is old. It's not like in Italy."
>
> (field notes, February 2019)

The area around the North station is home to an administrative centre (with skyscrapers and government buildings) at the front and some of the poorest and deprived neighbourhoods of Brussels at the back (Opbouwwerk Brussel, 2002). Here, categories of colour and class separate people geographically (Deboosere et al., 2009). As argued by Sanders, "In urban spaces [...] groups who are outside the mainstream are confined, or at least attempts are made to confine them to hidden shadows, away from a legitimate place in public and their rights to full citizenship" (2004, p. 1714).

Some carrés have been sealed as the result of ongoing police investigations and the purchase of some of the carrés by the government of Saint-Josse (personal communication stakeholders). Therefore, these abandoned buildings are not maintained and contribute to a general "deprived look". The researchers observed illegal dumping of garbage, odour nuisance, and broken windows of bars and carrés.

> "The place is dirty. They spit and pee on my pavement. We have to clean it before we start."
>
> (Roxy, field notes, June 2019)

On several occasions, the researchers saw women pouring water on the pavement and arduously cleaning their carré and the area outside it. This happened mostly between 6 pm and 7 pm, when the women started the night shift, and could be interpreted as a way through which the women maintain control of their environment and protect their dignity.

There is little institutional or governmental presence in the area, and the women expressed their apprehension during the interviews.

> Mary takes us to a bar, and we buy her a coffee. She wants to explain to us how things are in the area. "There is no love, no respect. People don't care about this area," she says. She is clearly frustrated.
>
> (field notes, February 2019)

The structural neglect adds to the frustration of the women as they believe that they are not treated fairly or with dignity. Espace P, an organization that supports the rights and well-being of sex workers is the only organization with a strong presence in the area. Their office is located in the district and the social workers regularly go on the streets and inside the carrés (to give the women lubricant gel and condoms, sometimes accompanied by a doctor). "Since 2013 we are purposely addressing the African women. This has been a slow and difficult process because most of them don't trust us," Teresa Tylova, a researcher and social worker of Espace P, explains (personal communication, February 6, 2019).

Although no official complaints are coming from residents about prostitution in the area of the carrés, Hélène Morvan explains that residents, including the women, might be discontented with the situation but do not think things can or will change. Often, they are unable to file their complaints through the official channels because they either do not understand how the system works, they lack certain skills (e.g. language), and/or do not trust the system (H. Morvan, personal communication, October 18, 2018). The place on the margin does not translate into political influence, which as Weitzer concludes about the Brussels situation, "allows the city to continue its policy of minimal engagement and tolerance of the status quo" (2014, p. 67).

4.1.3 Stigma

Peršak and Vermeulen argue that moral order tends to be spatially regulated in the urban setting (2014). Prostitution, or the act of offering sexual services in exchange for money, has defied conventional morality and family structures throughout most of history (Rodriguez Garcia, 2016). Prostitution is considered by many as threatening to the conventional order, and the term "prostitute" is often used to describe deviant behaviour of women. The accounts of the participants revealed experiences of stigma.

> "If they know what kind of job you do, they won't look at you," Stella replies when I ask her if she has any contact with Belgian nationals.
>
> (field notes, June 2019)

Stigma informs social attitudes towards prostitution, "fostering an environment where disrespect, devaluation, and even violence are acceptable responses to those who are stigmatized" (Benoit et al.,

2018, p. 460). In the red-light district of the carrés, women suffer harassment that is linked to the stigma of prostitution (personal communication stakeholders). Some women who work at night say that passers-by sometimes take photos, and the women find this very unsettling as they worry about what will be done with those photos.

> "Just yesterday there was an Arab woman that was taking pictures of the windows with her phone. It's not nice. They don't want us here."
>
> (Rose, field notes, June 2019)

Rose's reaction shows that this societal reaction generates a feeling of being unwelcome. Her quote also reveals intergroup tensions in the area, using "they" versus "us".

> Beauty is outside her window when we arrive. She tells us of a meeting that was organized in the area, but stresses that she did not go: "Of course I will not go, it is ridiculous that anyone would expect me to join a group meeting – as if prostitution is something I am proud of doing."
>
> (field notes, May 2019)

Beauty's quote illustrates how some of the women internalize the stigma of prostitution, as Beauty is ashamed of doing this kind of work. Her statement highlights one of the challenges of the empowerment approach employed by organizations like Utsopi who advocate for the rights of sex workers. In response to our question about where she goes to church, Celia answered:

> "How can I be doing this work and go to church? I pray yes, but I cannot go to church now."
>
> (Celia, field notes, March 2019)

In most parts of Nigeria prostitution is not accepted and is even considered a taboo,[4] and outside the carrés most of the women hide the fact that they work in prostitution. The sinful connotation that the women themselves attribute to prostitution, therefore, generates feelings of shame and guilt.

> "If any one of the girls ever sees me in Italy one day and says hello or asks me if I am not the one who worked in the carrés in Brussels, I will deny it because it is not something I am proud of."
>
> (Lulu, field notes, May 2019)

Both external and internalized stigma have an impact on the mental health and emotional resilience of women in prostitution (O'Neill et al., 2009). They can also affect the capacity of the women to fight for their basic rights. However, within the group of women from Nigeria and Ghana who work in the carrés, there are different attitudes towards prostitution, and there is also a minority who try to resist the stigma by employing a rights-based discourse.

"We are just doing our work, not bothering anybody. I have the right to do with my body what I want."

(Agnes, field notes, February 2019)

4.1.4 Insecurity

During the six months of fieldwork, security was the main topic of conversation. Almost all the women answered "security" or rather "a lack of security" to the question of what the biggest challenge in the area was for them. They referred both to the situation inside and outside their carrés.

Joma and Isabella say the clients can get aggressive, especially at night. They both have scars. Joma has one on the inside of her hands and Isabella points to her neck.

(field notes, May 2019)

"If they cannot improve it, they should close it down."

(Mary, field notes, February 2019)

The field notes demonstrate a sense of urgency about this theme, and the stakeholders confirmed that the area is very insecure with an increase in crime rates over the years. They state that the violence in the red-light district is not fundamentally linked to the prostitution activities but is regrettably often directed at the women.

"The criminality is new. I think it's been five years or something. We as women have nothing to do with it. It used to be full of clients. The cars were lined up. This has changed because the area is degraded and there's drug dealing. It's dirty and dangerous."

(Nancy, field notes, February 2019)

Especially at night, the darkness contributes to a disconcerting atmosphere. Some parts of the Linnéstraat/rue Linné and the

Plantenstraat/rue des Plantes are quite deserted as opposed to the busy Weidestraat/rue de la Prairie, where people on the street are visibly intoxicated, and men are gathered in small groups.

Observing the setting in which the women work helped to shed light on the potential risks. Although the fact that "feeling (in)secure" is a subjective experience, for which the stories are the most valuable sources of information, the researchers also felt the hostility/insecurity through the way they were looked at and approached by certain individuals.

Harassment

A large-scale study on prostitution in Brussels, carried out in 2008, observed that residents and merchants in the North quarter

> have clashed with the sex sector over three issues: (1) nuisances: traffic congestion, parking problems, noise, car break-ins, visitors' behaviour (e.g., offensive language, fights), (2) building owners who do not repair their buildings, and (3) the erotic image of the zone, which clashes with local Muslim sensibilities.
>
> (Seinpost Adviesbureau, 2008, in Weitzer, 2014, p. 59)

These factors are legitimate grievances of community members. Especially in densely populated areas, public prostitution is not easily compatible with other activities, both residential and commercial. "There are people who argue that residents should not complain because they knew very well that prostitution was taking place before they moved in the area," says one of the stakeholders. However, in the Brussels context where cheap housing is scarce, not everyone has a fair choice of where to live (É. Haquin, personal communication, October 18, 2018).

In the last two years, these grievances have led to an upsurge of direct harassment and intimidation of the women (personal communication stakeholders).

> "They throw eggs. Why would they make the effort to go and buy eggs to throw at us?"
>
> (Violet, field notes, May 2019)

Violet expresses her apprehension about how there are people who go out of their way to harass them for no reason, this is incomprehensible for her. It is unclear whether this is coming from residents of the area itself, or people coming from outside. The women say it is mostly Turkish men and children who cause trouble. On a few occasions during the fieldwork, the researchers witnessed men on the streets yelling insults at the women.

> Rose, who also works at night agrees: "The little boys are a problem. They are rude to us. They say 'fuck you' or make gestures at us. What kind of parents let this happen? It's a problem with the parents. The boys are only 14 or 15."
>
> (field notes, May 2019)

There are also acts of vandalism that lead to material damage and, commonly, windows are deliberately broken. During the six months of fieldwork, the researchers saw more than 20 broken windows. Some of the bars in the area were also attacked, and it became a recurrent topic of conversation.

> During the focus group, Maya addresses the others: "My window is broken again. It also happened two months ago, I had it fixed, and it just happened again. It's so expensive to fix."
>
> (focus group, field notes, May 2019)

Aside from the direct effect of the aggression, which is quite dangerous if the woman is standing right behind her window when it is smashed, it also has financial consequences, as the replacement of a window costs between 300 and 800 euros. Some women or landlords postpone the replacement, thereby contributing to the dilapidated feel of the area.

The clients are also targeted and the women blame the decrease of the number of clients (discussed earlier) on the decrease in security. They talk about "Turkish" or "Moroccan" men who pick on their clients.

> "The guys break car windows of customers. They steal from them. The Belgian clients don't come anymore after midnight. It's too dangerous."
>
> (Maya, field notes, May 2019)

> "I have seen the area change over the last ten years. Business used to be good. Clients came and went, Belgian and foreigners. Now, things are different. The Turkish guys who live here chase the clients away. They especially target the white men coming into the area."
>
> (Ani, field notes, January 2019)

The hostile atmosphere is similar to what has been observed in other urban settings where "sex workers experience intimidation and harassments from the communities where they work and sometimes live" (Sanders, 2004, p. 1705). Kinnell notes that, in the UK, "verbal abuse, spitting and throwing objects ranging from stones to fireworks and bottles are common occurrences" (2006, p. 148).

Physical violence

The violence in the red-light district is primarily an economically motivated violence (É. Haquin, personal communication, October 18, 2018). There is a lot of money circulating in the area because of the drug dealing, prostitution, etc. and this may attract desperate individuals.

> "A client paid to stay the whole night with me in my carré. In the morning he woke up and wanted to run off with my phone."
>
> (Roxy, field notes, June 2019)

> "They steal also. They steal from the whites and also from the girls. It happened to me once. They stole all my money. When I was in the other street, the one they closed, one man stole 1,800 euro from me while I was in the bathroom. 1,000 was mine and 800 for a friend, I have to pay her back."
>
> (Issy, field notes, January 2019)

Almost every participant in the research has had bad experiences with clients or those pretending to be clients who came with ulterior motives, most commonly, theft. In some cases, men threaten to use violence (with or without weapons), actually beat up the women, or scare them by saying that they would report them to the police as undocumented. Many of the research participants, especially those who work at night, confirmed that this had happened to them. The women also said that men often demanded their money back if they were unable to ejaculate in the agreed time. Kinnell (2006) identifies this as one of the four main trigger factors that can spark off violence from male clients of prostitutes (O'Neill et al., 2009).

> She says she once had a client who wanted something sexual that she didn't want to do. He removed the key from the door, and when she said no, he punched her in the face and gave her a black eye.
>
> (Isabella, field notes, May 2019)

Today we see Hilary for the first time. We ask her why we haven't seen her before now. "I haven't been around because a client beat me up so badly that I was unable to work. I only resumed work very recently."

(field notes, May 2019)

Lastly, some women also mention forms of sexual violence. They explain that some clients want to have sex without using a condom, even when the women do not want this.

Anjie explains, enacting the scene while she is speaking: "The client will tell us to turn around to take us from behind, but he does this so he can take the condom off unnoticeably."

(field notes, May 2019)

A feeling of lawlessness

"There is a sense of 'tout est permis' in the area," said one of the stakeholders (É. Haquin, personal communication, October 18, 2018).

"There is no security. It's like the police don't care about us. Sometimes we call the police when something happens. Those who answer the phone don't understand English or they don't take it seriously. If we are lucky and they show up, they will come after 45 minutes or one hour. The criminal would have left. Then they ask you for the description of the criminal, which clothes he wore etc., but it's too late."

(Mabel, field notes, January 2019)

Apart from the occasional police car passing by, there is no regular police presence on the streets. At night, there is only one patrol unit, which comprises two police officers on stand-by for the entire Brabant street district (in which the red-light district is located, and which includes the lively Brabantstraat/rue de Brabant and the Aarschotstraat/ rue d'Aerschot). When the women call the emergency number, it connects to the emergency calls central point in Brussels, not the station nearby, and they experience difficulties with being understood over the phone. Also, if the police do respond, they take a while to arrive.

"The police don't do anything. They just take our 'statement'. We don't want to give statements."

(Keke, field notes, January 2019)

The women generally have a straightforward understanding of justice. They expect a direct response from the police, meaning that they should come and arrest the person who caused harm on the spot. They are not fully aware of the complicated process of managing administrative complaints, and that this is often not as straightforward as they would like it to be. Many of the women perceive the justice system to work against them rather than for their well-being. Certain incidents, like that of 2018 New Year's Eve also serve to reinforce this. It was a particularly unsettling night (described in a field note at the beginning of this section) that left a deep impression on the women.

> "At some point, the police came there but they did nothing and just watched as these horrible things happened. Are these ones police officers?"
>
> (Didi, field notes, May 2019)

Almost everyone said that they wanted policemen in uniform on the streets. Other suggestions that were made by the women included installing camera surveillance or alarm buttons inside the carrés:

> When I mention Antwerp, Momo says that she would prefer it all to be official. "That they build something and that it is all in order [...] The police can protect us, and we can do our work with dignity."
>
> (field notes, May 2019)

In 2008, it was noted that some women working behind windows (in the whole North quarter) complained about a lack of police surveillance on the streets, especially on weekends (Seinpost Adviesbureau). Interestingly, one of the recommendations of that report, while looking at the success of the reorganization of Antwerp's red-light district, was to set up a police station in or near the area to ensure close observation and rapid reaction to any violence (Seinpost Adviesbureau, 2008). In 2018, a new police station was officially opened on the corner of the Weidestraat/rue de la Prairie, right on the edge of the red-light district, in front of the first carré. The new station is quite big and visible, so it creates a presence of its own. However, its presence is not reassuring to the women, as crime rates have only risen in the area.

> "I wish the police station would close and be moved elsewhere, because instead of its presence bringing comfort and some form of consolation and a feeling of safety, it has brought more violence and fear."
>
> (Jojo, field notes, January 2019)

The situation of lawlessness in the same street as a large police station is hard to comprehend for most of the women as they have an understanding of what the role of the police is, and believe that they should be there to protect them.

> "Everybody talks about Africa and things being bad there. But in Ghana and in other parts of Africa, you could never dare to walk in front of a police officer while selling or dealing drugs, never! That would be impossible, because you knew that what they would do to you would be horrible. Yet here, people do it all the time and attack you, but nothing happens."
>
> (Edith, field notes, May 2019)

On Tuesday morning, June 5, 2018, 23-year-old Eunice was found heavily injured on the sidewalk of the Linnéstraat/rue Linné 130 in Schaerbeek. The injuries eventually led to her death, and the murder has had an enormous impact on the women working in the carrés. It triggered a powerful emotional reaction (T. Tylova, personal communication, February 6, 2019) and, for the first time, the African women united to speak up about the insecurity in the area. There was a strike and a march to demand changes. More than one year later, there is a widespread belief that justice has not been done because nothing seems to have changed in the area. The randomness of the act makes the women believe that it can happen again, on any day, to anyone.

> "It's dangerous now. You can just be killed and nothing will happen."
>
> (Stella, field notes, June 2019)

Some journalists framed the story as one of human trafficking, of a poor African woman who was deceived into coming to Europe to be sexually exploited and found death (Romans, 2018). The fact that she was "randomly" killed by a local minor and the state of general insecurity in the area were only marginally addressed. In the weeks following the murder, some of the women saw the boy in the area and they were apprehensive.

> "When the Nigerian girl was killed, they didn't catch the killer. He just walked the streets. There is nobody here to protect us. If they cannot catch a killer, what will they do to a man that just beats me or steals from me?"
>
> (Gold, field notes, January 2019)

In marginalized urban areas where prostitution takes place "violence may be perpetrated by clients, pimps or managers, drug dealers, robbers, other sex workers, passers-by or sometimes residents, whose activities can sometimes tip over into vigilantism." (O'Neill et al., 2009, p. 43) We learned that the absence of police in the area of the carrés has created a security vacuum that is prone to this as we discovered that "unofficial" actors offer security to the women.

> "When I have an aggressive client and manage to get out, I will lock him inside the carré and run out for help. The black guys outside will come and throw the guy out immediately."
>
> (Joma, field notes, May 2019)

Joma was referring to some of the men of West-African descent that are usually hanging around the main crossroads in the district. Keke said that they are willing to pay a contribution fee for their safety. If the police don't offer anything of the kind, she reasoned, they were obliged to turn to other actors.

> "If I get in trouble, I have the number of some black boys I call, and they come to help. There is also a Moroccan guy that protects the girl that works at night. I pay him 50 euro every week so that they leave her alone and no one breaks my window."
>
> (Keke, field notes, January 2019)

Although in Keke's eyes she managed to get a reasonable "deal", paying for safety isn't voluntary for everyone. Several women mentioned that they had to pay a weekly or even a daily sum of "protection money" (around 10 or 20 euros). The following field note of a conversation that took place inside one of the carrés is revealing.

> "There's a Moroccan that asks for 10 euros from every girl every night in this part of the area," Edith tells us. Lucy, who is working, calls from behind the curtain: "I refuse, I will call the police before I pay that man." "The police will not come so you should pay them and save your life," Edith reacts.
>
> (field notes, May 2019)

In the eyes of the women, these men are more powerful, or at least more in control, than the police. However, the interests of these "vigilantes" are ambiguous, creating a complex and very fragile feeling of security. On the one hand, the women feel protected, but on the other hand, they pay out of fear of the repercussions of defiance. The following field note shows that there is a thin line between who is harassing and who is protecting the women.

"Remember that new woman in the Weidestraat?" Nancy asks the others, "She was not around when they came to collect the money on Saturday. She didn't know because she was just new. They broke her window just because she wasn't there at the moment they came to collect the money."

(focus group, field notes, May 2019)

"Although women may not rationally decide to enter prostitution, their responses to the daily hazards they face can be calculated strategies of coping and resistance" (Sanders, 2004, p. 1708), portraying resilience and ways to take control of their environment. Considering the lack of safety, the women develop tactics to cope with this on their own.

"I used to work in the carrés at night, but I don't want to do that again. It was horrible. Once, a client pulled a knife on me. Also, Moroccan men threatened me. God has been kind to me, and I was able to escape all the bad situations. Outside on the street, it's safe enough, but it's inside, when I'm alone with a 'client' or a 'pretend client' is when things get bad."

(Issy, field notes, January 2019)

Issy makes a risk assessment of the situation and concludes that it is more dangerous at night and inside the carré when she is alone. All the women we talked to confirmed that it is more dangerous to work at night, so, some simply chose not to work at night (like Issy did).

"I never work during the night. I stop around 6 pm and then I go home to Antwerp where I live."

(Ani, field notes, January 2019)

"At night the young girls work. They are stronger. I cannot do it."

(Jojo, field notes, January 2019)

The advantage of working behind the window is that it allows the women to screen clients. Research shows that women who have lengthy experience working in prostitution become experts in this (Kinnell, 2013; Sanders, 2005). Most of the women said that they refuse certain clients.

Pearl installed a side mirror next to her window so that she has a wider view of the street and can see who is coming. We test it out and it works. She can now anticipate who will otherwise suddenly appear in front of her window.

(field notes, June 2019)

"If they are drunk or if they've caused trouble before, I refuse to take them as clients. And when they come inside, they have to fully undress and put their clothes on a chair in case they carry weapons."

(Sally, field notes, March 2019)

If the client threatens to use violence, the women weigh up their options.

We ask the women what they do when customers ask for their money back. They all seem to agree on this: "You give it back! What will you do? The police will not help you, and if they break your window, it'll cost 500 euros to fix. So, in the end you'll lose even more money."

(focus group, field notes, May 2019)

In this case, they choose not to resist as a minimal form of agency. Similarly, Anjie explained that she has stopped getting braids or hair weaves. She prefers a wig because clients sometimes pull her hair.[5]

Women try to communicate with each other when something fishy happens, in particular with women in neighbouring windows. Some women knock on the wall, others leave open their curtain, and others try to phone. But that is not always successful, especially when the others are busy with a client.

Diamond tells us she's been sleeping inside the carré. She says the girl at night is happy with the company. "You know how many times I have helped her with crazy customers? They don't know that there is someone sleeping behind the curtain. If they get rough with her, I open the curtain and shout 'hey' with an angry look on my face. They usually leave immediately."

(field notes, June 2019)

In some cases, a woman is indeed not alone in her carré. A colleague, friend, or madam can be in one of the two rooms, often behind a curtain, not visible to the client but they can sleep or intervene when necessary. Several women said they feel safer when someone is with them.

> "Sometimes there was 'someone' in the back while I was working. The same way I would sometimes be in the back when the daytime person was working. That was good because if I ever got in trouble with a client, I could call them to help me fight him off."
>
> (Sally, field notes, March 2019)

Mabel tells us she only pretends someone else is in the room. "A man came. He asked me the price and I said 20 euros. He came in but he wanted me to lock the door behind. He wanted to rob me. I lied and shouted to my sister behind the door. There was nobody behind it but I pretended. What else can I do? There is no security here."

> (field notes, January 2019)

We discovered that making a scene can also be a tactic to scare bad clients away. It is used to draw attention from passers-by and other women, but also to embarrass or scare clients.

> "If a client dares to do something, I take off my wig and run around like a crazy woman. It works. They run away." She re-enacts the scene while she is describing it to us. The scene is very amusing.
>
> (Joma, field notes, May 2019)

In some cases, women say they will not hesitate to fight back. One woman mentioned she had a "weapon".

> "What should I be scared of? If a crazy client comes inside, I will beat him with my purse and run outside. I can fight, I am not pregnant."
>
> (Roki, field notes, April 2019)

> "In spite of the danger out on the streets, the most dangerous place is inside the carré. When you are alone with a client, you never know who is there for something more than just sex. But I know how to take care of myself and I will fight back if anyone tries something stupid."
>
> (Agnes, field notes, February 2019)

4.2 Prostitution and migration: the migratory condition and the African community

4.2.1 Legal status and access to services

The migration status of the women came up several times in con-versations and although the "dichotomy legal–illegal" (Agustín, 2006, p. 117) is generally preferred, the reality here is far more complex. The women have long- or short-term residence papers, citizenship, huma-nitarian visas, running asylum applications, etc. We also observed that many women have residence status in other European countries, and while they can freely move around in the Schengen area, they may only reside or work in their country of residence. Since prostitution is not legalized and officially qualified as "work", they are tolerated behind the windows in Brussels. However, the women don't easily find access to the public health care system and are denied fundamental citizens' rights. Furthermore, changes in migration laws, including those in other European countries,[6] also affect these women.

Access to rights and services

Research shows that tighter migration laws have increased the vul-nerability of certain migrant groups (Sassen, 2003), and this is also the case for Nigerian women in Europe (Olaniyi, 2011). It can lead to experiences of isolation and stress related to the fear of arrest (and deportation), even in the red-light district of the carrés. This is exacerbated in the cases of those with no legal residence status as they have limited access to (1) justice and protection, (2) work, and (3) health care.

First, we noted that the women have limited access to justice as the label "illegal" is often used interchangeably or confused with "criminal". "If they are undocumented, [...] they will not be treated as victims of abuse but as violators of the laws governing entry, resi-dence and work" Sassen argues regarding women in prostitution (2003, para. 23).

> "I have residence papers from France, so I speak some French. I can call the police when I am in trouble, they will understand. [...] Sometimes when they come, the girl who called for help ends up being arrested. The Moroccan guys taunt them saying 'I have a Belgian passport; I have Belgian papers; what do you have? Call the police, I am not afraid, nothing will happen'. This is harder on

the girls who work without papers because they know that they cannot call for help, and the guys know it too."

(Roxy, field notes, June 2019)

Many women confirmed what she says, saying that they do not report incidences of violence to the police. They also mentioned the language barrier that complicates their access to the police because the person who answers the phone when they call for help often only speaks French.

I asked Gold if she calls the police when she's in trouble. "The police? (laughing) They won't do anything, just ask for our documents." She seems to find our question amusing.

(field notes, January 2019)

"There was a white man who was very drunk and fell down hard. A policeman came, ran to get water and called his colleagues. If it was a black man, the first thing would have been 'give me your document'."

(Anjie, field notes, May 2019)

"Unregistered or clandestine prostitutes have always tended to be afraid of reporting cases of violence by customers, for they risk official punishment – and deportation in the case of illegal immigrant women" (Rodriguez Garcia, 2014, p. 41). This is not without reason. To report a crime or an act of (sexual) violence, the women explained that they have to submit their official ID, and this discourages them from doing so, especially if they are undocumented.

Second, the women cannot easily access the formal labour market. Some of them expressed their desire to do "another kind of job", however the labour market in Belgium has limited options. The women who work in the carrés are often constrained by insufficient knowledge of French or Dutch, no work experience that they can account for, a low level of education or education that is not highly valued in Belgium, and/or no valid work permit.

Usi calls me over and tells me that she needs a job. She says that she is really good at cleaning. While she says this, she is mopping the floor of her carré and about to begin work. She says she can work as a cleaner and will work really hard. We've known her for a while now so I ask if she has any documents and she says that she doesn't.

(field notes, May 2019)

The options of migrant women are often limited to cleaning jobs and domestic work, which can be burdensome, discriminatory, and very low-paid. Moreover, in case there is no official contract, the women are susceptible to labour exploitation. "Of all these informalized occupations, commercial sex pays the best," Augustín rightly argues (2006, p. 122).

> "The young ones, they just fight for their food and family. The girl that works here is a graduate in Nigeria, but she has no papers. What else can she do?"
>
> (Keke, field notes, January 2019)

> We ask Ani what she would do if the carrés close. She replies that she has stopped before, but she spent two years looking for another job. She went to school and got job counselling, but it didn't work out, so she came back.
>
> (field notes, January 2019)

Third, the women expressed their incomprehension of how the health care system works and their inability to access it sometimes. The way public health care is organized in Belgium is quite complex and individuals are covered by the system if they carry out the compulsory registrations, which have quite a complicated administrative process. Some women working in the carrés, especially those with Belgian residence status, are integrated into this system and do receive adequate care.

> "I am fine. I don't need anything. Also, medically, I am ok. I have my paper because I am married to someone from here, so I don't have those kinds of problems."
>
> (Roki, field notes, April 2019)

In contrast, a substantial number of women who were interviewed were not aware of where they could go with their health problems.

> "There is no help. I only go to the emergency room. But after, there is no follow up if you have no doctor. I don't want to go home to Italy. I went to OCMW, but they asked me to bring many documents."
>
> (Gold, field notes, January 2019)

In the field, the researchers were sometimes confronted with health-related struggles or needs, which highlighted that there was little access to formal services.

> The second lady who opens the door today asks what we are doing in the area. After we explain, she says she isn't feeling too good. She then proceeds to say that she can't hide from me the fact that she recently had an abortion and knows fully well that she shouldn't be back at work yet as her body needs to heal. However, she has been back at work since January and now feels pain in her womb. She feels the pain when she has a client and also when she doesn't have a client. It's constant and she is worried. She puts my hand on the side of my stomach because she wants me to feel exactly where it is.
>
> (field notes, February 2019)

Institutional and police distrust

In Nigeria and Ghana, which are countries that experience high levels of corruption, people learn to be cautious when it comes to authorities. During their migration trajectory to Europe, research shows that many of them were deceived (by traffickers) or abused by police officers (in transit countries) (UNODC, 2006). Finally, on arrival in Europe, the contact with government officials and the police evolves primarily around "having the right documents", and not around their equal participation in society.

> "You cannot trust the Arab police. They are like our police in Nigeria. They take bribes. They are together with the clients who attack us. If the policeman is Moroccan, he will start speaking Arabic with the guy and let him go freely."
>
> (Usi, field notes, May 2019)

In general, the women said that they do not trust the police to "be on their side" but this is also linked to their residence status. Johan Debuf, who is with the local anti-trafficking unit of the police, explains that in the past the focus of the local police was to chase illegal immigrants. Now they have shifted their focus, and building trust with the women is one of their priorities (personal communication, October 5, 2018), however, some damage has been done. Those who were around when the police focused on identifying the undocumented still fear the police and they tell the new arrivals.

"Not so long ago, we arrived in the carrés (in civilian clothing) and one of the women, when she saw us coming, ran out of her carré in flip-flops in the cold while we are just there to protect them."

(J. Debuf, personal communication, October 5, 2018)

"The young women have bad renting contracts, yet they don't come to us because they don't trust us," says Tylova (Espace P) (personal communication, February 6, 2019). The women who work in the carrés do not trust easily, not even staff of support services. This is also complicated by the fact that the women often do not speak one of the national languages, and are not familiar with local cultural codes or administrative procedures.

According to research conducted in several European countries, Weitzer (2014) discovered that women in prostitution are widely opposed to being registered by authorities for fear that this information could become public. Registration can offer benefits, but it also introduces forms of control (Rodriguez Garcia, 2014). The women who work in the carrés defy this by hiding, changing their names, and sharing documents. Research shows that distrust can be a tactical choice: a minimal form of agency and a way to stay in control (Simoni, 2013).

4.2.2 Little Nigeria

The majority of the African women working in the red-light district of the carrés are of Nigerian descent (more specifically from Edo state) with a minority originating from Ghana. These Ghanaian women all belong to the older generation of women who have been around for a long time. Most of the Nigerian women eat Nigerian food, watch Nigerian films, have Nigerian friends, and, if they go to church, attend a Nigerian church, and this is illustrative of the segregated lives that they live.

The Nigerian diaspora is made up of strong and valuable networks that spread all over Europe, maintaining close links with Nigeria, and these communities play an important role for newly arrived migrants in helping them to adapt to their new cultural environment. In the red-light district of the carrés, we discovered that the social relations the women forge are almost exclusively with other Nigerians as they share cultural norms, language, and migratory experiences that facilitate socialization. In addition, due to racism and the sometimes-hostile migration environment that exists in Belgian society, the community can offer a home-feeling that is very beneficial to the women. A few women told us that they attend Nigerian churches in Brussels or the city they live in, explaining that there is no scarcity of Nigerian churches for newly arrived women looking for a church to attend; whether they go, however, is a different story.

> "There are Nigerian churches everywhere. That is no problem. If someone new wants to go to church, someone else will show them the way."
>
> (Nancy, field notes, June 2019)

In the red-light district of the carrés, other economies co-exist with prostitution and attract Nigerians to the area, such as services that arrange money transfers to Nigeria, which is very important for most of the women who send money to their families. In the African shops, everything from toothpaste to palm wine to fresh avocados is brought directly from Nigeria, and cooks prepare meals (pepper soup, jollof rice, moi-moi etc.) that can be delivered to the women while they are working. There is a hair salon and an internal trade of clothes, make-up, jewellery etc. An observation made by the researchers during the fieldwork was that Nigerian politics or culture were often the topics of discussions in bars and shops.

Nigeria is also present in another way that should not be disregarded since most of the women own smartphones with which they stay in touch with friends and family members in Nigeria, and mobile Internet enables video calling which makes contact even more tangible. On a few occasions, the women were too busy on the phone and did not have time to talk to the researchers or the women passed their phone to the researchers to meet their boyfriends whom they were video chatting with. Via their phones, the women also read Nigerian news, watch Nigerian movies, and listen to Nigerian music. Window prostitution implies a lot of waiting time (Vandecandelaere, 2019).

For women who do not reside permanently in Brussels, diasporic networks also facilitate mobility between different European cities. If their stay is temporary, they allow the women to at least speak their language, practise their religion, and get familiar foods.

The women working in the carrés create alliances among themselves for different reasons: for protection, for company, and for practical reasons such as housing or arranging a workspace, and since most of the Nigerian women there originate from Edo state, they also share the same mother tongue. Some women expressed a sense of urgency to band together in response to their perception of a hostile environment.

"The people may not want us here, the police may not protect us, if we don't look out for each other, then who will?"

(Issy, field notes, January 2019)

Of the older generation of Nigerian and Ghanaian women (45+) who have legal residence status in Belgium, some have formally united. Following the death of Eunice in 2018, ten Nigerian and Ghanaian women went to the Nigerian Embassy and the local governments, demanding improved security measures in the area.

4.2.3 Transnational mobility

Mobility is an important theme with far-reaching consequences in the red-light district of the carrés. There is a high level of (1) inter-continental mobility, (2) mobility within Europe, and (3) movement within the red-light district itself. The women use this mobility to adapt to certain changes in their environment as forms of agency that may be both strengthening/liberating and unsettling/worrisome. It also influences the future that women envision for themselves.

For the women of Nigerian descent, Nigeria is still "home" and those who can travel and visit family, go on holidays, or do business, do so. Two of the participants travelled to Nigeria during the duration of the fieldwork because they lost a parent. The death of a parent is a very meaningful and important event in Nigeria and may put financial pressure on children, especially those who have migrated abroad, as the women themselves explained. This is because some family members expect them to contribute financially towards the funeral arrangements, which are often very elaborate.

Other women longed for their next trip home to see their loved ones, as some of them left their children behind in the care of family members. While this may be surprising or even frowned upon in Belgian society, it is not uncommon in Nigerian society, as families (including extended members) often work through life as one unit (Commisceo Global, 2020). Most of the women experience forms of immobility, due to strict migration laws, and as much as they would like to travel to Nigeria, are unable to.

While talking about her day, every now and again Pearl slips in an Italian word. She explains that she goes to Clemenceau (Brussels market) to do her *spesa*, meaning her groceries. She laughs, saying she sometimes genuinely forgets how it's said in English.

(field notes, 26 March 2019)

As this field note indicates, "home" for some of the women working in the red-light district of Brussels sometimes meant Italy, Spain, France, or even Greece. It is their first "host" country, where they know the language and have friends. In these three streets it is not uncommon to hear Spanish or Italian words, confirming that in general "the nature of migrant sex work in Europe is itinerant and transnational" (Agustín, 2006, p. 116). As we have described, the diasporic networks facilitate mobility and the women move across borders, following where there is money to be made, there is a space to work, and there is someone they know who can give them access to that space.

We noticed that the women also move in response to the financial crisis. Many of the women have moved from other European cities to Brussels to temporarily work in prostitution (J. Hendriks & F. Vandelook, personal communication, November 10, 2018). "Considering prostitutes engage in their work for money" (Peršak, 2014, p. 102), this is not surprising and means that today there is a constant "supply" of women to fill the carrés.

> I ask Stella what attracts women to come work in the red-light district in Brussels. "I think it's the money that attracts them. Here you can make money," she replies.
>
> (field notes, June 2019)

However, with the decrease in clients, the high cost of housing, and high rents of the carrés, the women are not always able to make the amount of money that they would like.[7]

> Although Lulu has only been around for a few months, today she tells us she is going back to Italy. "I am happy to be leaving. What's even worse is the fact that while I've been working here, I haven't been making any money because business is so slow and there aren't many clients around. I had to plead with the landlord to reduce the last rent because I couldn't afford to pay, and he took €100 off my bill."
>
> (field notes, May 2019)

Women also move in reaction to tightening prostitution laws. Roxy had recently come from France, where she was no longer able to work in prostitution legally (as a result of the 2016 abolitionist laws). Mary also explained her reason for moving to Brussels:

> "I came here six years ago from Spain. There was crisis you know, and racism. In Spain, when you are black you are a

prostitute. Here, at least when you leave this area, you can be anybody."

(Mary, field notes, February 2019)

The women challenge a system of integration programmes and social care for migrants based on national residence status and language-learning of the host country, as this is based on the premise that all migrants settle in the country. This research, however, showed that the women in question often consider their stay in Brussels a temporary one. They are focused on earning money and are not necessarily interested in investing in an overly comfortable lifestyle (with regard to housing, interacting with locals etc.) or exploring their surroundings. Some argue that prostitution attracts women because it offers flexibility and independence (Rodriguez Garcia, 2014).

"My plan is to do this for a few more years until I have saved enough and can set up a business back home in Edo state."

(Jojo, field notes, January 2019)

This access to mobility has another downside. The fact that open borders (within the Schengen area) do not translate into joint policies on prostitution, trafficking, or migration means that there is no uniform system of protection for the most vulnerable women, who are prone to exploitation. Madams sometimes move women around to keep them purposefully isolated and hinder police investigations (J. Hendriks & F. Vandelook, personal communication, November 10, 2018).

Some of the participants mentioned having worked in other Belgium cities, e.g. in the red-light district of Antwerp. One woman mentioned that she worked in a bar on the Aarschotstraat/rue d'Aerschot when there were still African women working in that red-light district. This is potentially relevant as it might explain the working regimes that some women have transported into the red-light district of the carrés: e.g. working in shifts instead of alone.

As noticed early on in the fieldwork, not all of the women working in the red-light district of the carrés have a fixed spot. The organization is adapted to the mobile lives of the women, and this system offers a lot of flexibility for some, but uncertainty for others.

When we meet Isabella on the street, we ask her how she is doing now that she has lost her carré-spot. "Soldier go, soldier come, after barracks go remain," she answers with a smile. She already has a new place to work and mentions that she earns more money there.

(field notes, May 2019)

4.2.4 Internal differences

Three groups

The African women who work behind the windows are by no means a homogenous group.[8] During the many interviews and conversations, the diversity among them became even more apparent. Although their place on the margin as black, migrant women working in prostitution may generate similar experiences, they are distinct individuals who relate to others in complex processes of identification. There are certain categories through which the women distinguish themselves, the most tangible being:

- *Age*: the women are aged between +/− 18 and +/− 60. There is a clear difference and separation between the "older generation" of women aged over 50 and the "new generation" of those aged between 18 and 30.
- *Origin*: the women were born in Nigeria or Ghana and uphold strong relationships with their country of origin. We only met one woman who was from another (to us unknown) African country.
- *Migration status*: the women have different long-term, short-term or pending residence statuses, which were issued by different European countries.
- *Family situation*: the women have different family situations regarding marital status and children. For those who have started their own family, family members may be living with them, or reside in another European country or in Nigeria.
- *Time in the area*: The women we met had worked in the red-light district of the carrés for the duration of one week to over ten years.

These categories influence the processes of group formation. While risking being reductive, this research can distinguish three main groups.

1   The first generation of women who arrived from the 1990s onwards. They are aged between 45 and 65 years old, of Nigerian or Ghanaian descent, live permanently in Belgium, and often have family members who live with them. Some of the women in the

group have joined Utsopi, a sex workers' collective in Brussels. Of the women quoted/mentioned in this book, we consider Kosi, Ani, Megan, Beauty, Lulu, Edith, Momo, Hilary, Bella, Erica, Didi, and Agnes as belonging to this group.

2   Young Nigerian women who work at night and have little "Europe-experience". They mostly live in shared houses or inside the carrés, and it was clear that there were potential victims of trafficking in this group. Of the women quoted/mentioned in this book, we consider Rose, Maya, Sally, Stella, and Usi as part of this group.

3   Women in their thirties and forties. They were trafficked but have paid off their debt and came from other European countries (mostly Italy and Spain) to work in the red-light district in Brussels. Of the women quoted/mentioned in this book, we consider Issy, Mabel, Gold, Jojo, Keke, Pearl, Diamond, Celia, Anjie, Joma, and Isabella as part of this group.

Some women, however, find themselves on the intersection of these groups. Roki, Violet, Lucy, and Roxy for example fall somewhere in between groups 2 and 3.

Intragroup tensions

During their time in the area, the researchers witnessed tensions between and within these groups. According to social identity theory, group conflicts are expressed through the comparison of individuals of one group with those of another: favouring one's group, exaggerating or generalizing certain aspects of the other group, and retaining only negative information of the other group (Turner, 1975). For example:

- The existence of negative stereotypes about Nigerians/Benin girls, especially expressed by women from Ghana.
- Older women think the presence of young women creates unfair competition.
- Women who have been working in the red-light district for a longer period were unwelcoming to newcomers, as the next field note illustrates.

"We have to do something about those refugees that come and take our place," Didi says, when she addresses the other women. She is referring to the women that arrived more recently from Italy and Spain.

(field notes, May 2019)

Some tensions are related to the stigma associated with prostitution, as younger women disapprove of older women in the profession.

Joma says she wants to make some more money before returning to Nigeria to marry and settle down. About the "older" women in the carrés, she says: "The women are so old and have been there for so long without shame. Most of them either have no kids, or have only one and most of the time, the father is either nowhere to be found, or unknown. We will not be like those women and will leave this lifestyle before we get to that age."

(field notes, May 2019)

There are circumstantial factors that create competition between the women and contribute to the tensions:

- There are fewer clients. This is a trend that is visible in all red-light districts in Belgium (Vandecandelaere, 2019) but reinforced by the current state of insecurity in the case of the red-light district of the carrés.
- There are fewer windows available. Over the last two years, a lot of the carrés have been closed.
- The legislation is not respected and there is ambiguity about who is allowed to "stand" behind the windows and work. Therefore, some of the women take advantage of this confusion to facilitate or block access for certain groups.
- The women experience constant pressure to earn money. While they do not have a fixed/guaranteed income, they need to pay the monthly rent and expenses of both their living and working places. In addition to that, many of them have become breadwinners for their families back home.

Turner showed that intergroup conflicts are biased and subjective, and on a deeper level serve to enhance one's self-esteem (1975). Research has shown that women working in prostitution are vulnerable to experience low self-esteem (Campbell & O'Neill, 2006). This vulnerability is intensified in the case of the African women who work in the carrés, because of

1 the assumption that most of these women have a history of being trafficked (see 4.3.4)
2 the prevalence of harassment from residents or passers-by

3   internalized stigma (see 4.1.3). Prostitution is considered morally deviant behaviour, also in Nigeria (Alobo & Ndifon, 2014) and Ghana (Awusabo-Asare, 2010 as cited in Lithur et al., 2014).

In this context engaging in conflict or avoiding it can be interpreted as a desperate way to enhance one's self-esteem.

We asked how they were and they told us that not long after we left two days earlier, a fight broke out and it was really, really bad ... the girls were talking about it and how it is so stupid that the women were fighting over some guy ... and that no guy is worth that.

(field notes, March 2019)

Today we see Beauty again. The first time we met her, she had just arrived in the area. We ask her if she's made some friends in the area. "I don't want contact with the other women. I don't need friends. I don't want to get involved in any trouble or fight," she replied.

(field notes, April 2019)

Beauty chooses not to "get involved" with the other women because, within two weeks of her arrival, she has already understood that this is a divided community that could cause her "trouble".

When we ask Celia what she would like to see changed in the area, she replies: "We are not together. If we could have one voice it would be good. If we would organize ourselves."

(field notes, March 2019)

4.3 Prostitution and policy: the modus operandi of the red-light district of the carrés

4.3.1 Local legislation

The joint approach on regulating prostitution-related activities in the red-light district of the carrés which was drafted by Schaerbeek and Saint-Josse in 2011 has been unable to reach a mutually beneficial result (see 3.2.3). Within the context of a politics of containment that accepts prostitution on its territory, its focus lay on improving the well-being of the women, eliminating pimping, and minimizing nuisance related to the activity. The police units responsible for anti-trafficking efforts (both on a federal and local level) are in favour of such an approach as they need the visibility that the red-light district offers, and argue that if prostitution goes underground it will be harder to detect the victims (J. Debuf, personal communication, October 5, 2018; J. Hendriks & F. Vandelook, personal communication, November 10, 2018).

From the Schaerbeek perspective, stakeholders identify several explanations for this failure: (1) priority was given to the red-light district of the Aarschotstraat/rue d'Aerschot (which was considered more urgent due to the unsanitary working conditions of the salons and the nuisance for the inhabitants) (É. Haquin, personal communication, October 18, 2018), (2) imposing the urban planning legislation of the carré, i.e. the fact that only the woman whose name is on the rental contract can work there, has proven to be challenging (J. Debuf, personal communication, October 5, 2018), (3) measurements to improve security have not been implemented (A. Vlaemynck, personal communication, October 5, 2018), and (4) the government of Saint-Josse has chosen to abandon the approach. Several of the stakeholders, however, expressed scepticism about the achievability of a workable solution.

Saint-Josse-ten-noode

In 2013 the municipality of Saint-Josse distanced itself from the joint approach to improve the existing red-light district. They instead researched the possibility of building a Brussels version of Villa Tinto (a large, regulated brothel in Antwerp), which is slightly removed from the area, but were unable to go through with it because the cost was too high (Vileyn, 2018). Instead, as explained by the mayor, Emir Kir, they have been making interventions in the area to curb prostitution activities to restore its residential character (Vileyn, 2018). This is in line with more global trends that "focus on the exclusion of prostitution from public spaces" (Peršak & Vermeulen, 2014, p. 15).

The government of Saint-Josse drafted new regulations, purchased properties[9] that contained carrés on the ground floor, and built a new complex that contains social apartments and a daycare centre. Several of the stakeholders indicated that this is not an apolitical intervention but one that was strategically carried out by the municipality in their bid to end prostitution on their domain, as visible prostitution in the presence of schools and other services for children is by law considered a disruption of public order. Although we found newly arrived women to be unaware of these changes, others who are long-term workers in the area are involved in fighting these interventions in court and accuse the mayor of trying to force them out of his municipality.

"The Turkish Burgemeester is causing trouble."

(Keke, field notes, January 2019)

"The Mayor has no right to try and enforce his beliefs and religion on us. This is Belgium and not Turkey. Why would he establish a crèche in the middle of the carrés, knowing fully well that the carrés have existed there for a very long time?"

(Agnes, field notes, February 2019)

Saint-Josse is facing resistance in its approach. The last two adjustments to the police regulations concerning window prostitution were appealed by a group of sex workers before the Council of State (the supreme administrative court in Belgium), which in turn led to the annulment of the regulations. This happened because some of its elements were considered disproportionate, e.g. prohibiting night work (2016) and the sudden closure of 40 carrés (2018), or irrelevant, e.g. the municipal's motivation of fighting human trafficking is considered a federal matter.

Celia says she took an active part in fighting the new regulations: "I am part of the group that contributed money to pay a lawyer to fight the decision of Emir Kir to close the carrés," she tells us.

(field notes, March 2019)

The annulment of the regulations has the inverse effect of creating a laissez-faire environment of "anything goes", as the certificate of conformity (see 3.2.3) is no longer required.

At the onset of the fieldwork, in January 2019, the last 12 carrés in the Rivierstraat/rue de la Rivière in Saint-Josse were closed (personal communication stakeholders), now delimiting the red-light district to only three streets and leaving women in search of a new place "to stand". However, the women adapt to the changes that are taking place.

"Some are on the streets, looking for clients, you will see. Then when they have a client they will ask another girl if they can go inside."

(Diamond, field notes, January 2019)

After losing her carré, Issy phones us to say that yesterday she went to work in a bar near Rogier, an area in Brussels where bar and street prostitution takes place.

(field notes, June 2019)

There are also many rumours and speculations:

"I know they will close it. I have a boyfriend, he is Belgian and he told me by 2021 they will close."

(Mabel, field notes, January 2019)

"The rumour is that it will all close by the end of December this year. But I don't think they will just close without giving us time to find other options."

(Celia, field notes, March 2019)

Schaerbeek

In the small stretches at the end of the Plantenstraat/rue des Plantes and Linnéstraat/rue Linné, where Saint-Josse unnoticeably ends and Schaerbeek begins, women need a certificate of conformity, as per the local regulations, to work in the carrés. This applies to 33 out of 96 carrés because the 33 carrés fall under the jurisdiction of Schaerbeek and its legislations while the remaining 63 carrés are on the domain of Saint-Josse, which no longer regulates prostitution on its domain.

To obtain the certificate, the women need to submit a long list of documents and fulfil certain requirements. While these measures are put in place to protect the women, they are often experienced differently by the same women for whose protection they were created. As the following field notes show, the bureaucratic application process and the limited flexibility of the certificate can be experienced as burdensome and inconvenient for the women.

"It's too difficult! They need so many papers from us. I don't understand why they are making things so difficult. At least on the other side (Saint-Josse), they leave you alone. You have to pay 250 euro just to start the procedure. But if you travel and you don't finish it, you need to start again, and then you have to pay again. And it's only me that's allowed to stand here. It's easier in Saint-Josse. Because here, if I travel for one month, I cannot put somebody else in my window. It can only be me. There you can change but it's full. There are no more carrés available in Saint-Josse."

(Bella, field notes, May 2019)

"It's a lot of work. Many documents, not only for me but also for my landlord. Many documents. You have to go, and then again, and then again. They ask a lot for this document, and also from the owner."

(Erica, field notes, May 2019)

In the nearby red-light district of the Aarschotstraat/rue d'Aerschot, women with a predominantly Eastern European migration background work in "salons". These are considered commercial premises that allow the sharing of workspaces and working in shifts. It is not easy to comprehend the existence of different legislations no more than 100 metres apart.

When we ask if she has any recommendations, Stella replies: "They should allow more girls in the same window. Like the whites in the other street. They are two or three. It makes sense, it's safer. The blacks can only stand alone. They are always one."

(field notes, June 2019)

Workplace requirements

The carrés in Schaerbeek have to meet certain safety measures (e.g. the requirement of a fire extinguisher), while there is no monitoring of the carrés in Saint-Josse due to the annulment of the local regulations (personal communication stakeholders). In addition, due to a "technical problem", Saint-Josse would not be able to impose certain material requirements that were put in the joint urban planning regulation for window prostitution. When the regulations were drafted in 2011, the carrés in Saint-Josse were already classified as carrés, as opposed to those in Schaerbeek, and this makes it legally impossible to impose the requirements. Inside the carrés, the researchers encountered a variety of situations. Some carrés are in good condition, while others are clearly neglected. However, the researchers did not observe a significant difference between the carrés in Schaerbeek and those in Saint-Josse, as the women take good care of the spaces that they have. Several of them put effort into decorating, and their carrés had coloured lights, posters on the wall, sheer curtains, wigs attached to the walls, sex toys on display, etc.

4.3.2 Informal regulation

The red-light district has evolved and transformed according to different dynamics other than intended in 2011, especially at night.

Prostitution activities are now organized in an informal and self-regulated way, filling a legislative vacuum that exists for different reasons, some of which have been earlier discussed:

1 Prostitution is not regulated on a national level.
2 Municipalities can only intervene on issues regarding public order and safety.
3 The local police regulations of Saint-Josse regarding prostitution have been annulled.
4 The local police regulations of Schaerbeek regarding prostitution are not imposed, especially at night.

Cost

The municipalities collect taxes on the carrés that are linked to their economic use. In Schaerbeek, this is around 1,200 euros a year and in Saint-Josse around 3,000 euros. The property owners set rental prices that also consider the commercial purpose of the premises and, from what the women told the researchers, the prices vary from 1,000 to 3,000 euros per month for the two rooms. Some women split the rental price in half while others pay a fixed amount or a percentage of their earnings per week or weekend. Although most women live elsewhere, for some, the carré is their home.

> Pearl is sleeping in the carré for the time being because she is trying to save up some money. She says that saving the €200 she used to pay as rent goes a long way.
>
> (field notes, June 2019)

The women say that they mostly charge around 20 euros per client, but this price may also be higher or lower depending on the type of sexual service performed, a specific (known) client, or the level of desperation they have to make money regardless of the amount when clients are scarce.

Flexibility

Most women in the carrés either work during the day or at the night. However, some rotate between night and day shifts (depending on what is available) or even do both at the same time. At night, young women come to the area hoping that there is a free window where they can work. One night, when the researchers were in a bar in the area, a young woman came in and word quickly spread that she needed a window to work in. Shortly afterwards, someone accompanied her out to show her the window where she could "stand".

Different roles

Women (and some men) in the red-light district have different roles with regards to prostitution: facilitating access, subletting, providing food and other services, arranging money transfers, security etc. Research has shown that migrant women who work in prostitution are generally dependent on intermediaries (Peršak & Vermeulen, 2014). This is also the case for other forms of informal labour, as "new-comers use the networks and the information of migrants who have arrived before them" (Wagenaar et al., 2017, p. 201). Newly arrived women explained that they came through a sister, an aunt, or a friend. The women depend on this intermediary to organize transportation, find a place to live in, and access a place to "stand"/work, and the women who have been in the area for a long time are the most knowledgeable on how to facilitate work for others. Many of the women who officially rent the carrés tend to unofficially sublet to others. Women who are no longer working in prostitution, and some men from outside of the African community, equally contribute to the facilitation of the activity.

> "We are helping them by giving them a place to work. They need to earn money to take care of their family."
>
> (Jojo, field notes, January 2019)

> It is afternoon and there are a lot of people outside. We are walking with Mary and a man stops her on the street, mentioning something about a contract. He is an older, Belgian man, and he asks us what we are doing in the area. I explain briefly, and then he says: "I help the girls. I have for a long time. Now that they've closed some of the carrés, some have no place to work. I help them. I make multi-tenant contracts. So they can share a carré with three instead of two. Where else can they go?"
>
> (field notes, February 2019)

Hierarchy

In her study in 2014, Tylova points out the asymmetric relationships and power differences between the women working in the carrés. She argues that their social status is determined by their origin, legal status, degree of autonomy, and age (2014). As a result, the organization of the prostitution activity has a certain hierarchical character. This is partly cultural because of the hierarchical culture of most African societies where age is believed to confer wisdom so older people are granted respect. The oldest person in a group is often revered and honoured, and in social situations they are greeted and served first. In return, they have the responsibility to make decisions that are in the best interest of the group. Status is further determined through someone's level of education, knowledge, motherhood, and wealth (Commisceo Global, 2020). During the fieldwork, how the women addressed the Nigerian researcher was exemplary. Depending on their position, they used the term "sister" (their equal or close in age) or "auntie" (deemed older or superior). These hierarchies (combined with family relationships) traditionally structure social order (Falola, 2001), of which there were obvious traces in the red-light district.

The women occupy different positions in the community, and this affects their level of agency. In the red-light district of the carrés, high levels of agency can translate into choosing when to work (night or day), being able to obtain a rental contract (and thus a stable and legal place to work), and having the option to sublet and generate an alternative income. Low levels of agency, on the other hand, mean that a woman only has the option to work at night (when it is less safe) and that she depends on others to have access to a carré, which gives little job security and makes her subject to fluctuating "stand" prices (and thus vulnerable to exploitation).

4.3.3 Sex workers support service

Espace P offers first-line assistance to sex workers, and although their services span all of the Brussels-capital area, including those working in private forms of prostitution, their office is conveniently located in the red-light district of the carrés. In the context of public health prevention, they offer free testing of STDs, give out condoms and lubricants, and provide gynaecologist consultations (T. Tylova, personal communication, February 6, 2019). They also provide referrals to the conventional health care system when needed. They can help evoke the procedure of Urgent Medical Aid, which is available for migrants without legal residence status but is difficult to access, or simply inform the women about how the health care system works (I. Jaramillo, personal communication, May 20, 2019).

Since 2013, Espace P has purposefully started addressing the women of Nigerian and Ghanaian descent with whom they formerly had no relations, having discovered as we did that building trust is crucial in reaching the women. On Tuesday evenings, one or two of Espace P's English-speaking social assistants go on the streets to establish contact with the women. In interviews, the women (who know about the services of Espace P) called it "that place", "those people", "Espace E" and "Payoka".

We ask them if they know Espace P or rather "those women that come around with condoms", which they usually understand better. All five of them say yes. They say they appreciate the fact that the women speak English and that they've gone there to get tested. "At least they try," Usi says.

(focus group, field notes, May 2019)

Despite their location, however, not all of the women whom the researchers interviewed were familiar with Espace P; this was especially true for the newly arrived women. They might have been given condoms, but often had not been to the office, which is discreetly located on the Plantenstraat/rue des Plantes.

Although the initial approach of Espace P is one of public health prevention, they are open to any questions sex workers might have and offer broader social assistance, which has proven to be very challenging. Tylova (Espace P) said:

"So let's say 7 years ago I started approaching women through a purely medical approach and only after 3 or 4 years I have been able to make some deeper connections with the older ones. But not with the young ones. And we know that administratively they are sometimes lost in the system."

(personal communication, February 6, 2019)

4.3.4 Malevolent exploitation and human trafficking

Migrants depend on "third parties to secure a job, a house, and to negotiate their interactions with the authorities, but this might provoke dependency and make them vulnerable to exploitation" (Wagenaar et al., 2017, p. 205). There are different "regimes of collaboration" in the red-light district, but we have little insight into the details of what these regimes entail. It is also difficult to judge the fairness of a financial agreement, especially those related to rental prices, as many of the women we met expressed some form of financial stress related to the high cost of working in the carrés.

The property owners charge high rental prices, thereby making it impossible or at least unrealistic for one woman to manage the rent on her own. It is not clear how this situation came about or what happened first: the increased rental prices (which motivated shift work) or the increased revenue because of carré-sharing (which made house owners/intermediaries ask more rent).

> "I pay 1,800 euros for my carré. It's beautiful. I am lucky. I sublet my carré during the night. The others do it, I didn't start it. How else can I afford to continue? The rent of my flat is another 850. With all expenses I have to pay 3,000 euros a month."
>
> (Megan, field notes, February 2019)

The fieldwork revealed indications that rent may on average be higher for the African women (+/− 2,000 euro) than for the Belgian women (+/− 1,000 euros). In addition, the taxes that are intended for the property owners are sometimes paid by misinformed women (Belgian sex worker, personal communication, February 16, 2019). The migrant women are vulnerable to exploitation when they do not have access to justice, or do not know exploitation is taking place. As Debuf stated in an interview: "The girls without a legal address in Belgium often have to pay more because they can't lodge a formal complaint for fear of the police" (personal communication, October 5, 2018).

"It was first Ghanaians who exploited Nigerians and later Nigerians exploiting Nigerians," Tylova explains (personal communication, February 6, 2019). Within the group of Nigerian and Ghanaian women, there are clear forms of malevolent exploitation. The existence of group conflicts and the hierarchical organization of the prostitution activities are not harmful per se but create an environment that is particularly unguarded and prone to abuse.

> Isabella has been told she can't work in the window anymore by the legal tenant of the carré. The woman told Isabella she isn't working enough and making enough money. Her friend Anjie tells us it's not fair because she can't help that there are not enough clients.
>
> (field notes, May 2019)

The issue of human trafficking was present in several ways, and while it was never the main topic of conversation, it often came up naturally in references and side comments that referred to the trafficked history of the women. A large majority of the African women of Nigerian descent in the red-light district originate from Edo state, the hub of human trafficking in Nigeria, and since legal migration pathways for many of these women are quasi non-existent, it may be assumed that most of the women who arrived in Europe irregularly went through a similar experience of trafficking. While many of them have "bought" their freedom and are free of their debt bondage, they carry a particularly violent past with them, which informs the choices and decisions that they make. Research shows the women are vulnerable to mental health issues that have been linked to trafficking: e.g. depression, anxiety, PTSD (Altun et al., 2017). Some of the behaviours that were observed in the carrés during the fieldwork which demonstrated anger, hostility, and irritability could result from these.

> From inside Beauty's carré, we can see a woman with a cut on her face, standing outside. We ask her what happened. Beauty tells us about a fight that took place. One woman had broken a bottle which she wanted to attack the other woman with but in the struggle, she ended up being the one who got hurt as the bottle slashed her badly.
>
> (field notes, May 2019)

During the fieldwork, the researchers made some observations that indicated potential cases of human trafficking as some of the younger women (estimated age between 16 and 20) refused to participate in the research. They looked frightened and were clearly being watched either by someone on the street, from behind another window, or from behind a curtain inside the same carré. The lawless atmosphere undeniably makes it an easy location for traffickers, especially at night.

> "I am trying to earn for myself, but there is too much competition from the Nigerian madams. Everyone knows what is going on in the area, including the police, but no one is doing anything about it. It would be better for the carrés to be shut down once and for all, that way none of them would be working and things would at least be fair."
>
> (Kosi, field notes, January 2019)

Tylova suspects that some women are at the same time victim and madam: "There are also victims that understand that they can pay off their debt faster by exploiting others and they do this for example, by subletting their carrés at night at a high price" (personal communication, February 6, 2019).

The anti-trafficking teams of the federal and local police, PAG-ASA and Espace P confirm the presence of human trafficking networks in the area. Recent cases (2014 and 2017), that were elaborately described in the Myria Year Report of 2018, inform us about how they operate:

- In the case of Madam J, the crimes of human trafficking took place between 2014 and 2016. According to the report, the network smuggled dozens of girls, including various minors, from Nigeria to Belgium and other European countries to exploit them into prostitution. They operated on an international level and moved the victims from one location to the other when they suspected detection by the police, and also exchanged victims between different madams in Belgium, Italy, Spain, and Sweden. The victims were recruited in Benin City, made to travel through Libya, and juju rituals were undertaken to ensure their loyalty in Nigeria and Europe. In Brussels, the girls were put to work in the carrés. This case reveals that "madams" or sponsors sometimes reside in other European countries, which makes them difficult to detect (Myria, 2018).
- Mama L. was arrested in 2017 for being involved in the exploitation of 56 Nigerian girls, some of whom she had helped to smuggle into Belgium. She previously worked in the carrés for many years and, by 2017, she was subletting about 27 carrés and making big profits (Myria, 2018). While the official communication said that 30 victims had been rescued, 25 of them were arrested and released with a letter ordering them to leave the country. The case is interesting because it illustrates how immigration agendas sometimes outweigh victims' rights (Campbell & O'Neill, 2006). These are experiences that potentially leave their mark and influence future interactions with the authorities.

4.4 Four challenges

After describing the experiences of the Nigerian and Ghanaian women in relation to the complex social-political context, we must now ask the question: what does this tell us? It is clear that the unsettling and chaotic context in which the women work presents numerous challenges to them. However, as we have discovered, the group of African women is not a homogenous one. Within this migrant group of women, there are different "generations" that relate to the host society and migrant community in distinct ways, and their well-being is subsequently conditioned by other priorities and interests. Nevertheless, we were able to identify certain "problems" that some or all women struggle with daily. In the following section, we will list the most prominent difficulties and examine how they successfully or unsuccessfully cope with them. Revealing these dynamics is important when thinking about possibilities for change or gaps in support services. We can identify four main difficulties:

4.4.1 Security

The public–private character of window prostitution makes women extra vulnerable to violence because sexual exchanges happen inside, where the women are mostly alone with a client. The windows that offer them the visibility necessary to solicit clients connect the women with their direct surroundings: the streets, residents, and passers-by, etc. The women described countless accounts of harassment, thefts, and violence, both inside and outside their carrés. As mentioned earlier, the main concern of all participants is that they feel unsafe in the area and that they feel insufficiently protected by the police whom they don't always understand (language barrier) or fully trust, mainly because of their slow responsiveness and little presence. They subsequently don't report the violence which they experience and sometimes turn to other actors for protection.

The women have developed tactics and strategies to protect themselves: they keep each other company, they keep "weapons", they pay for protection, they scare clients away, they fight back, etc. and these are effective ways to prevent robberies or rape from taking place. However, they cannot prevent all forms of violence and the subjective experience of insecurity creates a lot of stress for them. For a group that normally prefers to stay away from any kind of authority, the plea for police presence in the streets is remarkably strong.

4.4.2 Health-related issues

Some of the women are unable to access basic health care services. For women in prostitution, which in its nature implies a lot of health risks, access to health care is primordial. Most of the women did not understand how the health care system works in Belgium, especially those who do not have legal residence status in Belgium. Although many of them had met the Doctor from Espace P, not all of the women knew about the organization or made use of their services. Also, when referred to other services (like a general practitioner), not all of the women followed up on the referral. While this may be linked to language barriers, we also hypothesize that it is partly cultural. The women mentioned that in Nigeria it is unusual for someone to go to the hospital alone when they are ill as they are usually accompanied by a family member or friend. The information on reproductive health and safe sex is also necessary for the women because many of them are not educated enough in this area (T. Tylova, personal communication, February 6, 2019). Within the Nigerian and Ghanaian community, the women help and inform each other. However, the information that is passed on is not always correct and there is no guarantee that everybody is sufficiently cared for (due to high mobility and internal exploitation).

4.4.3 Work-related stress

One of the main issues that the women were preoccupied with was money. They complained that the rent was too high and that there were not enough clients to earn the amount of money that they wanted, and some expressed the difficulty of making ends meet (covering their monthly expenses). We believe this contributes to a competitive atmosphere and tensions within the group as the women (sometimes literally) have to fight for their spaces and the clients. The findings also showed that certain regulations and political decisions caused concerns as the confusion and uncertainty about the future of the area made some women very angry. Finally, two other factors that contribute to their stress "at work", but are more related to their migratory condition, are the lack of access to other types of work and the fear of deportation by those who are undocumented.

4.4.4 Discrimination and (perceived) stigma

Closely related to the security issue, there is also the more subjective experience of "not being welcome". Most of the participants gave at least one or more examples of situations or events that occurred in which they experienced stigma or a form of discrimination, including their encounters with the police.

The most upsetting experience for the women is the harassment by children and young people, who throw eggs at them or break their windows. These attacks by children go unpunished and leave profound impressions on the women. The women also revealed their internal

conflict about working in prostitution, and several of them expressed
feelings of guilt and shame about it as prostitution is not considered a
respectable profession in Nigerian society. It is important to note,
however, that a minority among the women are tackling the stigma by
joining a collective that supports the rights of sex workers.

The material setting in which the red-light district is located also
fuels the experience of "not being welcome". Drawing on Hayward,
Di Ronco rightly labels the area as a perfect example of a "space of
deprivation" (2014, p. 149), located on the margin of the urban and
political space and neglected by institutions. Most of these women
find comfort in the Nigerian and Ghanaian community that offers
company and familiarity, especially those who feel less "at home" in
Belgium. The transnational networks of Nigerian and Ghanaian
communities in other parts of Europe make it possible for the
women to move easily across borders.

Notes

1 Eunice was a 23-year-old Nigerian woman who was murdered in June 2018
   outside her carré.
2 The use of verbatim quotations in this book allows for the most direct and
   unfiltered access to the voices of the women. However, interviews were
   never recorded, and the quotes used here are taken from the field notes.
   Some sentences are literal recollections, while others merely rehash the
   essence of what was said. To improve comprehensibility, the texts are
   somewhat adjusted and sometimes translated into English (mostly from
   Nigerian Pidgin), staying as close as possible to the original. Finally, all
   names are fictionalized, and some personal information was omitted to
   guarantee the full anonymity of the participants.
3 There is also a presence of residents that have a Roma background, but it is
   unclear how the women perceive them.
4 The Edo (Bini) ethnic group traditionally does not socially accept prostitution
   (see Alobo & Ndifon, 2014).
5 This not only hurts but touching someone's hair without permission is also
   culturally very inappropriate for black women. As expressed by Mokoena:
   "do I let people touch my hair and under what circumstances? The question 'can I touch it' becomes one of the most awkward social moments and
   can break relationships before they start" (2018, para. 2). Also see Dash
   (2006).
6 According to a controversial new decree in Italy, issued by the government on
   September 24, 2018, humanitarian protection was abolished. Since 2011,
   many Nigerians who came through Libya obtained this type of protection, as
   did some of the Nigerian women who work in the carrés. It is not clear what
   will happen when it is time to renew their permit (every one or two years).
7 The issue of rent is a complex and contradictory one. It is not clear how
   much rent the house owners ask for a carré, because some of the sum is

handed over unofficially (Myria, 2018; J. Hendriks & F. Vandelook, personal communication, November 10, 2018). More importantly, it is not clear what the standard should be of a reasonable rent. In Belgian law, asking a disproportionate rent is criminalized. House owners argue that the space is used commercially, which allows them to demand more rent. Was subletting first or the increase in rent? What incited the other?

8 Tylova made a distinction between two main groups of women in her ethnographic research in the area (2014), those from Ghana and those from Nigeria. Within the group of Nigerians, she highlights the diversity of experiences.

9 By 2019 the municipality had bought a total of 21 buildings of which the ground floor was used as a carré (MdK, 2019).

References

Agustín, L.M. (2006). The conundrum of women's agency: Migrations and the sex industry. In R. Campbell & M. O'Neill (Eds.), *Sex Work Now* (pp. 116–140). Willan Publishing. doi:10.4324/9781843926771.

Alobo, E., & Ndifon, R. (2014). Addressing prostitution concerns in Nigeria: Issue, problems and prospects. *European Scientific Journal*, 10(14), 1857–7881. doi:10.19044/esj.2014.v10n14p%25p.

Altun, S., Abas, M., Zimmerman, C., Howard, L.M., & Oram, S. (2017). Mental health and human trafficking: responding to survivors' needs. *BJPsych international*, 14(1), 21–23. doi:10.1192/S205647400000163X.

Benoit, C., Jansson, S.M., Smith, M., & Flagg, J. (2018). Prostitution stigma and its effect on the working conditions, personal lives, and health of sex workers. *The Journal of Sex Research*, 55(4–5), 457–471. doi:10.1080/00224499.2017.1393652.

Campbell, R., & O'Neill, M. (2006). Introduction. In R. Campbell & M. O'Neill (Eds.), *Sex Work Now* (pp. ix–xxi). Willan Publishing. doi:10.4324/9781843926771.

Commisceo Global (2020, January 1). Nigeria – Language, Culture, Customs and Etiquette. https://www.commisceo-global.com/resources/country-guides/nigeria-guide.

Dash, P. (2006). Black hair culture, politics and change. *International Journal of Inclusive Education*, 10(1), 27–37. doi:10.1080/13603110500173183.

Deboosere, P., Eggerickx, T., Van Hecke, E., & Wayens, B. (2009). The population of Brussels: A demographic overview. Synopsis, CFB No. 3. *Brussels Studies. The e-journal for academic research on Brussels*. https://journals.openedition.org/brussels/891#ndlr.

Di Ronco, A. (2014). Regulating street prostitution as a public nuisance in the "culture of consumption": A comparative analysis between Birmingham, Brussels and Milan. In N. Peršak & G. Vermeulen (Eds.), *Reframing Prostitution: From Discourse to Description, from Moralisation to Normalisation?* (pp. 145–171). Maklu. doi:10.1080/13876988.2015.1013760.

Falola, T. (2001). *Culture and Customs of Nigeria*. Greenwood Publishing Group.

Gsir, S. (2017). Les nouveaux migrants à Saint-Josse. *EYAD asbl.* http://www.eyadasbl.be/wp-content/uploads/2018/07/Rapport-Les-nouveaux-migrants-%C3%A0-Saint-Josse.pdf.

IBSA. (2016a). Zoom sur les communes: Saint-Josse Ten Noode. https://www.ccc-ggc.brussels/sites/default/files/documents/graphics/fiches-communales/2016/saint-josse-ten-noode_fr.pdf.

IBSA. (2016b). Zoom sur les communes: Schaerbeek. https://www.ccc-ggc.brussels/sites/default/files/documents/graphics/fiches-communales/2016/schaerbeek_fr.pdf.

International Organization for Migration. (2015). World migration report 2015. Migrants and cities: new partnerships to manage mobility. https://publications.iom.int/system/files/wmr2015_en.pdf.

Kinnell, H. (2006). Murder made easy: The final solution to prostitution? In R. Campbell & M. O'Neill (Eds.), *Sex Work Now* (pp. 141–168). Willan Publishing. doi:10.4324/9781843926771.

Kinnell, H. (2013). *Violence and Sex Work in Britain.* Routledge.

Lithur, N.O., Williamson T., Chen A., & MacInnis, R. (2014). *Designing a Stigma and Discrimination Reporting System: Assuring Justice for People Living with HIV and Key Populations in Ghana.* Futures Group, Health Policy Project.

MdK. (2019, April 24). Saint-Josse: Six immeubles anciennement occupés par des carrées accueilleront des logements. *DH.* https://www.dhnet.be/regions/bruxelles/saint-josse-six-immeubles-anciennement-occupes-par-des-carrees-accueilleront-des-logements-5cc03e0d7b50a602945a8a8e.

Mokoena, H. (2018, February 24). From slavery to colonialism and school rules, navigating the history of myths about black hair. *Quartz Africa.* https://qz.com/africa/1215070/black-hair-myths-from-slavery-to-colonialism-school-rules-and-good-hair/.

Myria. (2018). Jaarverslag Mensenhandel en mensensmokkel 2018: Minderjarig, in hoogste nood. https://www.myria.be/nl/publicaties/jaarverslag-mensenhandel-en-mensensmokkel-2018-minderjarig-in-hoogste-nood.

Observatorium voor Gezondheid en Welzijn van Brussel Hoofdstad. (2015). Welzijnsbarometer. Brussels armoederapport 2015. https://www.ccc-ggc.brussels/sites/default/files/documents/graphics/rapport-pauvrete/welzijnsbarometer2015.pdf.

Olaniyi, R. (2011). Global sex trade and women trafficking in Nigeria. *Journal of Global Initiatives: Policy, Pedagogy, Perspective,* 6(11), 111–131.

O'Neill, M., Pitcher, J., & Sanders, T. (2009). *Prostitution: Sex work, Policy and Politics.* Sage Publications. doi:10.4324/9781843926771.

Opbouwwerk Brussel. (2002). Omgevingsanalyse en programmalijnen. https://samenlevingsopbouwbrussel.be/wp-content/uploads/2017/02/Ts-76-Opbouwwerkgebieden.pdf.

Peršak, N. (2014). Economic factors of prostitution: Money, nature, crisis. In N. Peršak & G. Vermeulen (Eds.), *Reframing Prostitution: From Discourse to Description, from Moralisation to Normalisation?* (pp. 101–119). Maklu. doi:10.1080/13876988.2015.1013760.

Peršak, N., & Vermeulen, G. (2014). Faces and spaces of prostitution. In N. Peršak & G. Vermeulen (Eds.), *Reframing Prostitution: From Discourse to Description, from Moralisation to Normalisation?* (pp. 14–24). Maklu. doi:10.1080/13876988.2015.1013760.

Renovas. (n.d.). Stadsvernieuwingscontract Brabant-Noord-Sint-Lazarus. https://www.renovas.be/home/herwaardering-van-de-wijken/brabantnoord-si nt-lazarus-2018-2022-home/Perimeter-359/.

Rodriguez Garcia, M. (2014). Prostitution in world cities (1600s–2000s). In N. Peršak & G. Vermeulen (Eds.), *Reframing Prostitution: From Discourse to Description, from Moralisation to Normalisation?* (pp. 25–51). Maklu. doi:10.1080/13876988.2015.1013760.

Rodriguez Garcia, M. (2016). Ideas and practices of prostitution around the world. In P. Knepper & A. Johansen (Eds.), *The Oxford Handbook of the History of Crime and Criminal Justice* (pp. 132–154). Oxford University Press.

Romans, S. (2018, June 7). Het trieste lot van de vermoorde Nigeriaanse prosti- tuee Eunice (23): prooi van haar pooister. *De Morgen*. https://www.dem orgen.be/nieuws/het-trieste-lot-van-de-vermoorde-nigeriaanse-prostituee-eu nice-23-prooi-van-haar-pooister~b0f24d490/?utm_source=link&utm_mediu m=app&utm_campaign=shared%20content&utm_content=free.

Sanders, T. (2004). The risks of street prostitution: Punters, police and protesters. *Urban Studies*, 41(9), 1703–1717. doi:10.1080/004209804200 0243110.

Sanders, T. (2005). *Sex Work: A Risky Business*. Willan Publishing.

Sassen, S. (2003, August 20). A universal harm: Making criminals of migrants. *openDemocracy*. https://www.opendemocracy.net/en/article_1444jsp/.

Seinpost Adviesbureau. (2008). Prostitutie Brussel in Beeld. https://adoc.pub/p rostitutie-brussel-in-beeld.html.

Simoni, V. (2013). I swear an oath. Serments d'allégeances, coercitions et stratégies migratoires chez les femmes nigérianes de Benin City. In B. Lavaud-Legendre (Ed.), *Prostitution nigériane: entre rêves de migration et réalités de la traite* (pp. 33–60). Karthala.

Turner, J.C. (1975). Social comparison and social identity: Some prospects for intergroup behaviour. *European Journal of Social Psychology*, 5(1), 1–34. doi:10.1002/ejsp.2420050102.

Tylova, T. (2014). La construction de l'identité sociale des personnes prostituées d'origine africaine à Bruxelles [Unpublished master's thesis]. Université libre de Bruxelles.

UNODC. (2006). Measures to combat trafficking in human beings in Benin, Nigeria and Togo. https://www.unodc.org/documents/human-trafficking/ht_ research_report_nigeria.pdf.

Vandecandelaere, H. (2019). *En vraag niet waarom. Sekswerk in België*. Epo.

Vileyn, D. (2018, May 16). Emir Kir steeds repressiever tegen prostitutie [Emir Kir increasingly repressive against prostitution]. *Bruzz*. https://www.bruzz. be/samenleving/emir-kir-steeds-repressiever-tegen-prostitutie-2018-05-16.

Wagenaar, H., Amesberger, H., & Altink, S. (2017). *Designing Prostitution Policy: Intention and Reality in Regulating the Sex Trade.* Policy Press.

Weitzer, R. (2014). Europe's legal red-light districts: Comparing different models and distilling best practices. In N. Peršak, & G. Vermeulen (Eds.), *Reframing Prostitution; From discourse to description, from moralisation to normalisation?* (pp. 53–69). Maklu. https://doi.org/10.1080/13876988.2015.1013760.

5   Conclusions and recommendations of the ethnographic study on Nigerian and Ghanaian women working in Brussels' red-light district

This book is the result of ethnographic research about the Nigerian and Ghanaian women who work in prostitution in the red-light district of the carrés in Brussels in 2019. The need for the study arose from a context that caused societal concern: several cases of human trafficking and a general security problem in the area, which resulted in the murder of a young Nigerian woman in June 2018.[1] Schaerbeek, the local municipality, and other actors working in the area, have expressed their concerns and a willingness to "care". From a human rights perspective, the challenge now is to show this "care" in a way that will adequately benefit the well-being of the women.

For six months, two researchers took an ethnographic approach to the field, made observations in the area, and conducted interviews with the women. In addition, they talked to several stakeholders who have long-standing experience in the area. We designed three main questions to which this research sought to find an answer. These questions are very broad in an attempt to allow a holistic approach to the subject and eliminate any pre-existing assumptions.

1   How do Nigerian and Ghanaian women working in prostitution experience the red-light district of the carrés? To understand anything about the experiences of the women, it was necessary to see things from their perspective. This came from the belief that including the voices of those on the margin will lead to a more complex and truthful understanding of social problems. In the results, we describe how the women perceive, experience, and adapt to three contextual realities: the setting where the red-light district is situated, the diasporic community which they are a part of, and to the specific prostitution legislation that exists.

2   Which difficulties are they faced with and how do they manage them? We discussed the difficulties that the women are faced with

while living and working in this setting and examined the impact that some of these issues have on their well-being. The four main challenges we were able to identify were: security, health-related issues, work-related stress, and discrimination and (perceived) stigma. We also discovered how, when faced with these issues, the women use their agency to actively protect their well-being.

3   Which changes could potentially be made to increase their well-being? A careful analysis of the results revealed a more complex understanding of the problem and this serves to formulate adequate recommendations to policy and practice.

Although the research project is locally situated in the red light district of Brussels, its findings and recommendations can be highly informative for other European settings where Nigerian women work in prostitution. As we have discovered, the women easily move across European borders to work and live elsewhere and literature confirms the presence of Nigerian women in prostitution all over Europe; however, evidence on the presence of Ghanaians is largely missing. Notwithstanding, urban poverty, areas of deprivation, discrimination, and violence against migrant women, elements that characterize the red light district in Brussels, are issues that can be found globally and possibly determine the working conditions of those working in prostitution.

5.1 Main conclusions

5.1.1 The social, cultural, and economic fabric of the area in which the red-light district of the carrés is situated is complex, marginalized, and conflict-filled

Twenty years after the Belgian politician Serge Patoul called the area an insult to its citizens (Brusselse Hoofdstedelijke Raad, 1998), it remains to this day a very problematic neighbourhood. There is a high density/concentration of marginalized and poor residents and users of the space. The presence of commercial activities, such as bars, drug dealing, and prostitution, also makes it a place with high mobility. There are tensions between groups with different ethnic backgrounds. In shaping how prostitution is experienced the "social backgrounds and political capital of the population residing in the vicinity" (Peršak & Vermeulen, 2014, p. 19) is very influential. The area is dirty, and the buildings are not well maintained, there is conflict, harassment and overt crime daily, and there is a tension between the commercial and residential character in the area. The fact that there are two local governments with two different policies on prostitution is confusing and results in a situation of lawlessness. The structural neglect of the area and its people have unfavourable effects on the women who work behind the windows.

5.1.2 There is a lack of security for the women

Prostitution is a high-risk activity that exposes women to different forms of violence. In the setting of the red-light district of the carrés, there is a high prevalence of physical, emotional, and sexual violence directed at the women. Stigma and discrimination furthermore result in everyday harassment: breaking windows, spitting, taking photos, etc., and the women are also frequently robbed. Fundamentally, there seems to be a breach in the basic code or understanding of prostitution, namely "the provision of sexual services for money or its equivalent" (Harcourt & Donovan, 2005, p. 201). One of the most common "problems" in the carrés is the presence of men who do not want to pay for the sexual services they receive. Since the police do not have a presence on the streets and are slow in responding to the women's calls for help, the women do not trust the police "to be on their side" and rarely report acts of violence or access the justice system. It is this security-void that has given rise to worrying vigilantism practices. Although the women have developed tactics for their survival, they cannot prevent all violence from taking place and the subjective experience of feeling insecure on an everyday basis is destructive for their well-being.

5.1.3 The experiences and needs of Nigerian and Ghanaian women in the red-light district of the carrés are diverse

The women share a similar migratory condition. They were born in West-Africa and migrated to Europe, where they carry the double stigma of being an immigrant woman and a prostitute. However, their experiences are very heterogeneous.

The distinction made into three groups is generalizing but helps to understand some of the complexities that we encountered. The first group identified are older Nigerian and Ghanaian women who work during the day and have legal residence status in Belgium. The second (and more recently arrived) group are Nigerians, mostly in their thirties, who were trafficked into Europe and have lived a considerable time in another European country (mainly in the South). They mostly come to Brussels for economic reasons and stay for a short or long time, working during the day and/or at night. The third and last group is made up of very young Nigerian women who work mainly at night. They have a lower status in the community, thus have less agency, and are more likely to be present-day victims of trafficking.

The women define their well-being according to different categories/ measures. First and foremost, while all the women work in the windows to make money, the reasons behind it are very diverse. Some are more individually motivated, others more related to the well-being of the family or community back home. They also relate differently to the host society and have different prospects and intentions in Belgium. Some women are attached to other European countries, which they consider more as their "home", or see their future in Nigeria, and this has implications for integration processes and language learning in Belgium. Finally, the women are individuals who have their own motivations and aspirations. Some for example want to have children, while others do not.

Between these groups, there are internal hierarchies that create a welcome order (in a very chaotic setting) but have the potential to become exploitative, especially in this context of deprivation. It is general knowledge that within Nigerian human trafficking networks, some women who were previously victims of trafficking themselves begin exploiting other women. Also, more "innocent" practices of exploitation or facilitation, e.g. subletting according to the Yemeshe principle, can be unreasonable and become malevolent. Although these hierarchies are not necessarily harmful, they do offer challenges to practitioners. While it is important to respect a certain group culture to gain trust and get access, some of the women may block or prevent access to others.

How the women perceive prostitution is also not the same. Those who disapprove of prostitution suffer internalized stigma and do not identify/relate to the labour rights discourse. In contrast, a small group expresses the desire for more recognition and respect for the kind of job they do.

5.1.4 There is a group of women "on the move" for which support services are not adapted and accessible

Most of the participants do not see Brussels or Belgium as their home, as they spent many years in their first country of arrival in Europe, only moving to Brussels for economic reasons. Some of these women have legal residence status in Italy, Spain, or even Greece, and do not necessarily plan on spending a long time in the red-light district of the carrés.

This is also because many of the women do not see prostitution as a long term "job" but as a temporary money-making venture, after which they hope to restart their lives in Nigeria or elsewhere in Europe. Therefore, these women are not necessarily interested in integration into the host society. Furthermore, due to strict migration laws, they prefer to move around unnoticed, to protect their freedom of movement. This high mobility does not facilitate the work of health and social workers and police in building trust relationships and protecting the most vulnerable.

Certain women thus fall outside of the law, and thus often outside of protection and care. This is a risky situation when it comes to women who work in prostitution and are therefore very vulnerable to different forms of violence, both malevolent exploitation and health risks, as they do not have access to the justice system. Support services play a vital role in offering low-threshold and confidential first-line support, as well as doctor visits inside the carrés and social work outreach. In Brussels, the health and social workers of Espace P, a very small organization responsible for offering support to all sex workers in the Brussels region, cannot sufficiently address the needs of the women.

5.1.5 The current policy frameworks regulating the carrés do not address the needs of the women

The legislation of the carré is not correctly implemented or applied as most of the women are unaware of or confused about the legislation, and the area is organized in a self-regulatory and informal way.

Regardless of the political (un)willingness to do so, we argue that this is foremost a consequence of the inadequate and outdated character of its design. Remembering the basic premise of the carré, i.e. that one woman (and one woman only) officially rents and works in the carré, it is clear from our findings that this is no longer adept to the situation of the main public working there, more specifically the African women. The mobile, insecure, and self-regulatory character of the area today generates the failure of this model. Research shows that prostitution markets are very flexible and constantly changing, therefore holding on to a model that once worked can be counterproductive for the well-being of those who work there.

In the 1980s and 1990s, this conception of the carrés could be considered ideal to avoid nuisance. This is important when taking into account the residential character of the area because it eliminated the need for any third-party involvement, as the women did not need anybody else in order to work. This last point is also important because it meant that the women were less vulnerable to malevolent exploitation. This worked well for the Belgian women (and still works for those who are there).

Today, however, the situation is different. First, the problematic nuisance in the area is mostly related to drug dealing and bars, which attract "disorderly individuals" (Weitzer, 2014, p. 59). The residential character might be threatened, but not by prostitution alone. Second, the rental prices have gone up because of exploitative rental practices and heightened competition for places. Third, the Nigerian and Ghanaian women have different needs, especially related to their migratory condition:

- The women are dependent on others to access a place to work (migrant condition).
- The women do not feel safe alone.
- The pressure to make money is higher because the women are often the providers for their family.
- The women travel and prefer a more flexible system.

These needs do not easily fit into the "one woman per window" model that does not allow double shifts, company, flexible contracts, or third party involvement.

5.2 Implications and recommendations for policy and practice

A critical implication of this research is the recognition of the complexity of the area in which the red-light district is located, and the heterogeneity of the group. This strikingly fits into Hayward's categorization of "spaces of deprivation" (Di Ronco, 2014, p. 149), typical of gentrified post-industrial urban spaces found all over Europe. There are no clear-cut or easy solutions to most of the problems encountered and it is important to take into consideration the many differences within the group of African women and the complex socio-cultural fabric of the setting in which they work. Since prostitution does not fall under one clear authority in Belgium as in most European countries, different levels of governance (justice, well-being, urban planning, etc.) must collaborate according to a collective vision that puts the well-being of the women at its centre. Failing to do so may cause the actions and policies of these different bodies to (un)intentionally hinder the progress of each other.

Building trust with the women is key to the successful outcome of any intervention. This is particularly challenging and will always be part of an on-going and labour-intensive process. It is important that the police and practitioners are honest about their intentions and adopt culturally sensitive and non-judgmental attitudes in their interactions with the women. However, there are important "issues" that complicate interaction with the women. First, the fact that the area is insecure, especially at night, hinders the work of practitioners as they also have to pay attention to their safety (Harcourt et al., 2010). Second, the presence of human trafficking networks inevitably impedes access to women who are being exploited. Third, although isolation and distrust are often developed as survival strategies and are not necessarily considered "problematic" by the women, they do interfere with attempts to reach them and provide support.

5.2.1 Community empowerment and revaluation of the area

It is unthinkable to contemplate real change for the women if nothing about this setting changes. Its current place on the margin does not translate into the political influence, which "allows the city to continue its policy of minimal engagement and tolerance of the status quo" (Weitzer, 2014, p. 67). We identified three major issues that contribute to the deprivation of the area and create social tensions that transcend the prostitution activity alone. For real (and necessary) change to take place, genuine investments have to be made to ensure that the area is a safe and clean place for all to reside and work in.

First, there is a dense population, resulting from the co-habitation of different socio-cultural groups with low socio-economic status, which sometimes leads to tensions between these groups. In this highly diverse context, in which there is little trust in the police and formal governance systems, and where there is a reliance on informal support structures, people emphasize real or perceived boundaries between themselves and others, which may have significant consequences for feelings of community, safety, and belonging. There is however little institutional interest in the area to deal with these tensions or address the social exclusion in general, but we believe that interventions aimed at improving social cohesion and addressing the grievances of the residents are necessary. This can be done by initiating partnerships and projects with socio-cultural organizations or empowerment initiatives on a community level. Besides, engaging cultural mediators and street workers in the area could have beneficial outcomes.

Second, there is tension between the residential and commercial character of the area. Bars, prostitution, and drug dealing undeniably disrupt a peaceful living environment to a certain extent. To address this, we recommend that overt signs of nuisance, especially violence related to drug dealing or public alcohol abuse, are closely observed and met with rapid reactions from the police and practitioners.

Third, illegal garbage dumping, vandalism, and bad odours unfavourably influence the sense of dignity of those who live in or move through the area. This could be improved with regular maintenance and cleaning and interventions that revitalize the public space. The general revaluation of the area is closely related to the security issue. According to Wilson and Kelling's famous broken windows theory, visible forms of crime and vandalism (in the urban context) can be interpreted as signs of little social and institutional control, thus inviting more informal and criminal activities (1982).

5.2.2 Security

We cannot sufficiently stress the urgency of addressing the (in)security issues in the area. To this end, it is first and foremost important to develop and implement culturally competent and respectful policing strategies that will not turn into the harassment of the women and their clients. We therefore strongly recommend the provision of appropriate training for police officers and members of law enforcement as well as the use of cultural mediators/interpreters' services when necessary, seeing the social and cultural complexity of the group.

In the short term, a safety protocol to prevent violence and facilitate the process of reporting crime should be developed for the women working in the carrés. This would require more police presence in the area, especially at night. The women themselves ask for the regular patrolling and presence of police in uniform in the area and we believe that this could directly disrupt the "lawless state" of today and eliminate some of the violence. Unlike the current situation, in which the women have indicated that it takes 45 minutes or more for the police to arrive after a crime has been committed, there should be a faster response system. This will in turn help to build and re-establish the women's trust in the police.

In the long term, other security measures should be put in place after careful consideration and in dialogue with the women working in the carrés. Examples of these are the instalment of alarm buttons inside the carrés that attract attention outside or the instalment of functional security cameras on the streets. These are two of the measures that were suggested by the women themselves. Also, we strongly advise the creation of a simple and straightforward complaint procedure for victims of physical and sexual violence that can also be made anonymously without fear of deportation or retribution. Inspiration could be taken from the M. (Meldpunt Misdaad Anoniem), that came into existence in the Netherlands in 2002 along the lines of the crime stoppers concept that is implemented in the UK and the United States. After all, the safety of the women and the value of human life should take priority over immigration concerns.

5.2.3 Support services

Support services in Brussels are highly understaffed and insufficiently funded to deal with all the complexities of this group. Pitcher highlights the challenging work that prostitution support/sex work services have globally; considering that the "group" of men and women working in prostitution is very heterogeneous, with very different needs (Pitcher, 2006). While the holistic and non-judgmental attitude of the health and social workers of Espace P is effective, due to the small number of staff the support they can offer is very limited. It is fundamental that extra funding and support are provided to the support services and partnering organizations to increase and maintain accessible and non-discriminatory first-line support services. This is necessary to reduce the risks related to prostitution/migration including social exclusion, health-related issues, and malevolent exploitation.

The accessibility of services that provide free and anonymous basic (health) care is essential and can be increased by extending the opening hours and expanding outreach initiatives on the streets by doctors and social workers, including at night. Taking into account the mobility and precarious situations of some of the women, consistent and high-intensity outreach work is very important, and this predominantly requires a lot of human resources.

Considering the low education level of many of the women working in the carrés and insufficient knowledge of reproductive health and sexual safety, it is important to invest in sexual health education and promote the use of condoms and contraceptives to prevent HIV and other sexually transmitted diseases (STDs) and pregnancy. Having discovered the high mobility rate of the women, this is a continuous and ongoing process.

Next to the (necessary) focus on healthcare, assistance and advice regarding other aspects that shape the well-being of the women must be more proactively available. These could be issues like housing, social networks, education, or legal advice and, in this case, on-ground social workers are key in gaining trust and providing referral when necessary.

Learning from the Brussels' experience, we believe that a possible partnership with NGOs more adept in dealing with migrants in transit would be beneficial, e.g. for the exchange of expertise and services related to healthcare and information on migration law. Alongside them, cultural mediators could be key figures in reaching the women more effectively, by both commissioning them to work on the ground or for consultations based on their expertise.

5.2.4 Legislation

Including the women in the decision-making process is essential. However, we are hesitant about contemporary theories that suggest collaborative governance (Wagenaar et al., 2017) or self-regulation with quality standard (Vermeulen, 2007) for the red-light district of the carrés, considering the internal hierarchies and forms of internal exploitation that take place within this particular group of Nigerian and Ghanaian women. Rather, we suggest the development of adequate regulations based on a better understanding of the lived experiences and needs of the women (through research and dialogue), and the (respectful) monitoring of these regulations, to detect forms of malevolent exploitation.

We believe that the two municipalities concerned here (Schaerbeek and Saint-Josse) need to collaborate to create common regulations for the red light district of the carrés. The area is made up of merely three streets and the municipal border is neither visible nor known to most women. The existence of different regulations is confusing for the women, therefore it becomes more difficult for both governments to implement these regulations. The Brussel-capital region could play an important role in this process of negotiation.

We recommend that the current regulations in Schaerbeek, based on the use of the certificate of conformity, are evaluated and adapted to the African public. Although this requires further reflection, we advise that the legislative model of the carré be revisited to allow more than one shift a day and to factor in the women's mobility. Clearer policies that are more realistic and desirable will be easier to implement and monitor, thus creating more room for NGOs and police to intervene to tackle the problematic issues in the area like the trafficking networks, various forms of violence, and social exclusion.

5.2.5 Anti-trafficking measures

This research has shown once more that combating the Nigerian trafficking networks must happen on a European level. Per the UN

Protocol against trafficking and 2017 European Commission Communication on the follow-up to the EU Anti-Trafficking Strategy (2012–2016), the EU should continue to promote and facilitate collaborations between police forces to do so. We also recommend a joint European policy on the reception and protection of victims, that guarantees the basic human rights of all victims.

At night there is no doubt that women who have been trafficked are forced to work in the window of the carrés. This urgently calls for a more proactive approach to the detection of victims. Clients, women who work in prostitution, health and social workers, and police all have an important responsibility to do so. Specialized anti-trafficking centres (like PAG-ASA in Belgium) should be more closely involved in the process, most importantly for their expertise in the complexities of victimhood, e.g. when women do not recognize themselves as victims. Also, considering the involvement of the family or larger community and the use of juju, we argue that not all victims are able to denounce their traffickers. Yet, in Belgium this is a prerequisite for receiving protection, as in most European countries. These women should be protected, addressed with dignity, and enlightened on what their rights are. Anti-trafficking measures should never lead to the detention of victims of trafficking, which is a regular practice.

To break the logic of internal exploitation – some women who work in prostitution start exploiting others – we believe that it is important to offer realistic job alternatives to women who want to (albeit gradually) quit prostitution. Women who are tired of working in prostitution often have not developed other professional skills and experiences and are not entitled to unemployment benefits or pensions because of the informal nature of prostitution. This makes them easily tempted to continue in the "business" in the same way they were once introduced to it – through exploitation. A lot of these women have been able to obtain legal residence status and, therefore, specialized projects (that take into consideration the complexities of the target group) could be set up to create alternative careers. Equally, sensitizing initiatives that are directed at the Nigerian and Ghanaian women working in the carrés, informing them of the legal and psychosocial consequences of human trafficking of themselves and others, are currently non-existent. These could be developed through the involvement of NGOs like Casa Rut or Piam Onlus in Italy, both co-run by Nigerian former victims of trafficking who over the years have become spokeswomen dedicated to ending human trafficking from Nigeria.

5.2.6 *Further research*

The field of prostitution is a highly under-researched one, yet to address and counter existing policies that are often merely based on ideological opinions and moral preferences, it is important to provide information about the actual state of affairs and continue high-quality and in-depth analysis. In the red-light district of the carrés in Brussels, we believe further research will contribute to a more complete understanding of the highly complex social, economic, and political fabric of the area. We list the most important below.

- The research was predominantly focused on the well-being aspect of Nigerian and Ghanaian women working in the red-light district. There is a lack of data on the quality of life of the women "outside of work": housing, social networks, leisure time, level of integration, etc. Although there is little distinction between the private and public lives of many of the women working in the carrés, more knowledge about this is essential to arrive at a comprehensive assessment of their well-being.
- The interviews involved asking the women about their subjective well-being and provided limited knowledge of a more objective assessment of their mental and physical health. This is necessary to inform health-related policy to provide the appropriate and adequate support to the women.
- This research clearly shows that there are tensions and hostilities between different actors in the area. Through the eyes of the women, however, it gives an insight into their perception of the local actors (social groups, police, etc.) and how they experience discrimination and corruption. To fully analyse the social dynamics in the red-light district of the carrés, it would be necessary to examine the experiences and perceptions of all the other actors who live in or are present in the area: the residents, the clients, the "troublemakers" (those who harass the women), etc. What are their experiences and possible grievances?
- The research and theorization of possible exit strategies would be important: What if the red-light district of the carrés closes? Where will the women go? What could be done to make this process more humane?
- Further research should be conducted on the relation between local prostitution policy and the working and living situation of Nigerian and Ghanaian women working in prostitution in other European cities. Comparison can be drawn between the settings to inform more effective policies.

Note

1 The idea of the SWIPSER study already existed: the study was being written at the time of the murder.

References

Brusselse Hoofdstedelijke Raad. (1998). Bulletin van de interpellaties en mondelinge en dringende vragen. Vergadering van donderdag 28 mei 1998. http://www.weblex.irisnet.be/data/crb/biq/1997-98/00034/N/images.pdf.

Di Ronco, A. (2014). Regulating street prostitution as a public nuisance in the "culture of consumption": A comparative analysis between Birmingham, Brussels and Milan. In N. Peršak & G. Vermeulen (Eds.), *Reframing Prostitution: From Discourse to Description, from Moralisation to Normalisation?* (pp. 145–171). Maklu. doi:10.1080/13876988.2015.1013760.

Harcourt, C., & Donovan, B. (2005). The many faces of sex work. *Sexual Transmitted Infections*, 81, 201–206. doi:10.1136/sti.2004.012468.

Harcourt, C., O'Connor, J., Egger, S., Fairley, C.K., Wand, H., Chen, M.Y., Marshall, L., Kaldor, J.M., & Donovan, B. (2010). The decriminalization of prostitution is associated with better coverage of health promotion programs for sex workers. *Australian and New Zealand Journal of Public Health*, 34(5), 482–486. doi:10.1111/j.1753-6405.2010.00594.x.

Peršak, N., & Vermeulen, G. (2014). Faces and spaces of prostitution. In N. Peršak & G. Vermeulen (Eds.), *Reframing Prostitution: From Discourse to Description, from Moralisation to Normalisation?* (pp. 14–24). Maklu. doi:10.1080/13876988.2015.1013760.

Pitcher, J. (2006). Support services for women working in the sex industry. In R. Campbell & M. O'Neill (Eds.), *Sex Work Now* (pp. 256–283). Willan Publishing. doi:10.4324/9781843926771.

Vermeulen, G. (2007). European quality labels in prostitution as an illegal sector. In G. Vermeulen (Ed.), *EU Quality Standards in Support of the Fight Against Trafficking in Human Beings and Sexual Exploitation of Children* (pp. 274–278). Maklu. doi:10.1080/13876988.2015.1013760.

Wagenaar, H., Amesberger, H., & Altink, S. (2017). *Designing Prostitution Policy: Intention and Reality in Regulating the Sex Trade*. Policy Press.

Weitzer, R. (2014). Europe's legal red-light districts: Comparing different models and distilling best practices. In N. Peršak & G. Vermeulen (Eds.), *Reframing Prostitution; From discourse to description, from moralisation to normalisation?* (pp. 53–69). Maklu. doi:10.1080/13876988.2015.1013760.

Wilson, J.Q., & Kelling, G.L. (1982). Broken windows. *Atlantic Monthly*, 249 (3), 29–38.

Index

For Product Safety Concerns and Information please contact our EU
representative GPSR@taylorandfrancis.com
Taylor & Francis Verlag GmbH, Kaufingerstraße 24, 80331 München, Germany

*9 780367 745561 *